MORE THEMATIC ACTIVITIES

for

BEGINNERS IN ENGLISH

MORE THEMATIC ACTIVITIES

for

BEGINNERS IN ENGLISH

Tosha Docherty & David Macdonald

Illustrations by Erik Millette

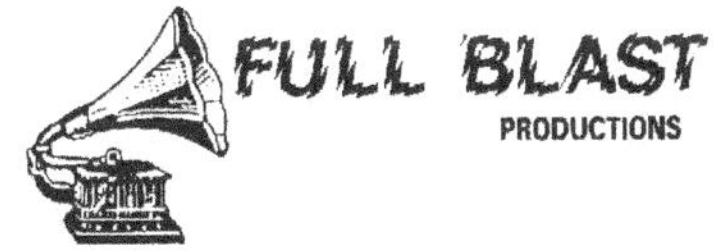

IN CANADA: IN THE UNITED STATES:
FB Productions   FB Productions
Box 408   Box 1297
Virgil, Ontario   Lewiston, New York   14092-8297
L0S 1T0

Canadian Cataloguing in Publication Data

Docherty, Tosha, 1966-
    More thematic activities for beginners in English

ISBN 1-895451-30-2

1. English language - Textbooks for second language
learners.* 2. Vocabulary - Problems, exercises, etc.
I. Macdonald, David, 1967- II. Millette, Erik.   III. Title

PE1128.D62 1997   428.2'4'076   C97-932590-0

Illustrations by Erik Millette

ISBN 1-895451-30-2

Printed in Canada

TABLE OF CONTENTS

INTRODUCTION

This reproducible book of ten thematically linked units is intended for learners who are just beginning to learn English. The idea behind the book is to ease learners into their new language through the use of illustrations and popular word games and activities.

Each unit of THEMATIC ACTIVITIES FOR BEGINNERS introduces twenty-four (twenty-six for The Alphabet unit) arbitrarily chosen vocabulary words on topics commonly taught to beginners. The book is designed to take a student from the introduction of the new vocabulary through a series of graded activities.

Each unit starts with a page of numbered SENTENCES. Each vocabulary word is used in a sentence. The sentences aim to use the words in an everyday context. Teachers are encouraged to use realia, photographs, their acting skills or any other stimuli along with these sentences to introduce the new words.

Following is a DRAWINGS page of the vocabulary words depicted pictorially. The drawings are numbered to correspond with the sentences on the previous page. The drawings are labeled, and below each drawing is a line on which the student can practice writing the vocabulary words being studied. Also, the drawings page can serve as a handy reference tool when completing the other activities.

The next page features the same illustrations laid out on the page in a different order. This time the DRAWINGS are labeled, but the letters of each vocabulary word are scrambled. The student must unscramble the anagrams to write the word.

In the next exercise, ORDERING, the student is given a list of the vocabulary words and must put the words in alphabetical order.

The QUIZ requires the student to respond to both questions about the vocabulary words in the unit and general knowledge questions about the topic of the unit.

In the DASHES exercise the vocabulary words are listed, but there are letters missing from the words. Each missing letter is represented by a dash. The student must complete each word by adding the missing letters.

A WORD SPIRAL follows. Each word is on the spiral. The student must circle the vocabulary words.

In the SCRAMBLES exercise, which is a Jumbles type exercise, the illustrations next to each example is a clue to the solution of the puzzle. The answers to the puzzles are taken from the SENTENCES at the beginning of the unit.

In the WORD MAZES exercise the illustrations are again used as clues to the solution of the maze. The illustration next to the START of the puzzle depicts the first word of the maze, while the illustration next to the FINISH of the maze depicts the last word required to complete the maze.

In the cloze part of the MAGIC WORD exercise the sentences used are the same as the ones at the beginning of the unit. This provides repetition of the words used in context. Again, the illustration provides a clue to the solution of the puzzle.

The EIGHT MISTAKES puzzle, although related to the topic of the unit, requires the student to use more vocabulary than that taught in the unit.

There is a CROSSWORD PUZZLE which uses the illustrations as clues.

The FIND-THE-WORDS PUZZLE has the student search to recognize letter patterns and the spelling of the vocabulary words.

The final page of drawings can be used as a TEST PAGE.

Finally, there is a complete ANSWER KEY at the end of each unit.

Teachers may choose to have the students work in pairs or small groups for some exercises.

Teachers may choose not to use all of the activity sheets in a given unit.

This book can be used with other thematically linked materials, but it has been designed to stand alone.

Unit 1: In The House

SENTENCES

1. I hang my clothes in the closet.
2. The old man was tired, so he sat in a chair.
3. He records his favorite television program on his vcr.
4. My father uses the computer to write letters.
5. My mother relaxes on the couch after dinner.
6. We keep the dishes in the cupboards.
7. Forks, knives and spoons are types of utensils.
8. I opened the curtains to let the sunshine in.
9. She sleeps with the lamp on because she has scary dreams.
10. My brother listens to loud music on his stereo.
11. My pillows are soft.
12. We had guests for dinner so we put out extra plates.
13. My mother puts the milk in the refrigerator to keep it cold.
14. He only watches television to get the news.
15. I walk up the stairs to go to my bedroom.
16. When clothes are dirty we put them in the washer.
17. Don't touch the stove when it is hot.
18. My family eats breakfast at a table.
19. My older sister is always talking on the telephone.
20. Before I eat, I wash my hands at the sink.
21. She prefers to cook her food in the microwave because it is very fast.
22. I have to use the toilet because I drank a lot of water.
23. I sleep in a bed.
24. Until we bought a dryer, we used to hang our wet clothes on a line.

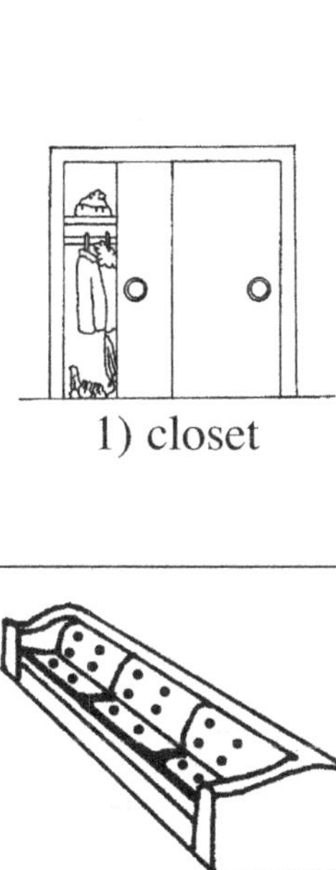
1) closet

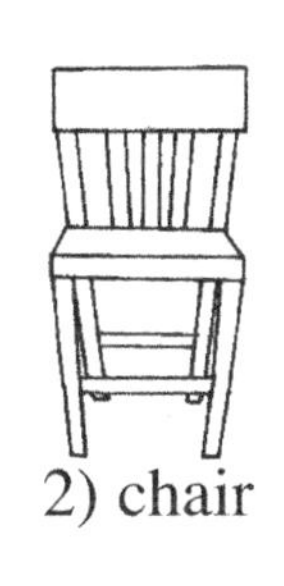
2) chair

3) vcr

4) computer

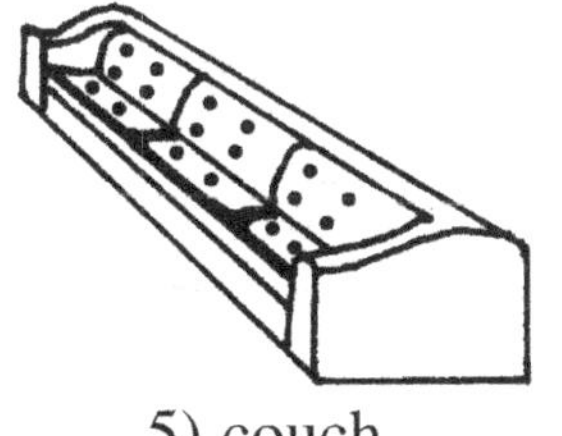
5) couch

6) cupboards

7) utensils

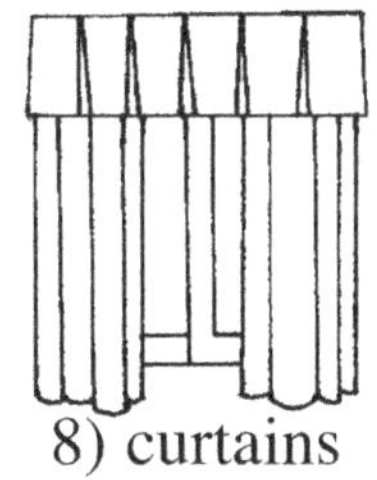
8) curtains

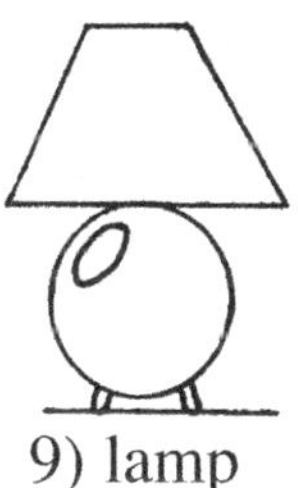
9) lamp

10) stereo

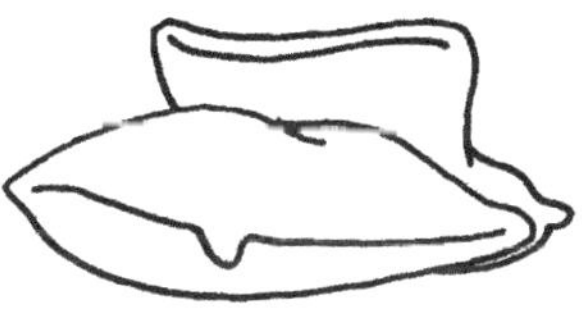
11) pillows

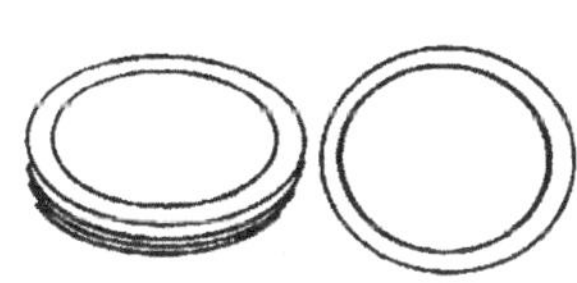
12) plates

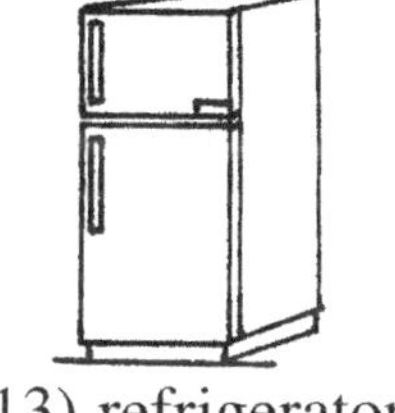
13) refrigerator

14) television

15) stairs

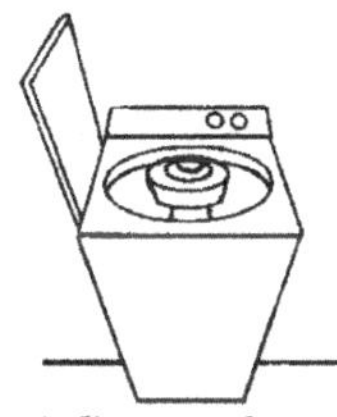
16) washer

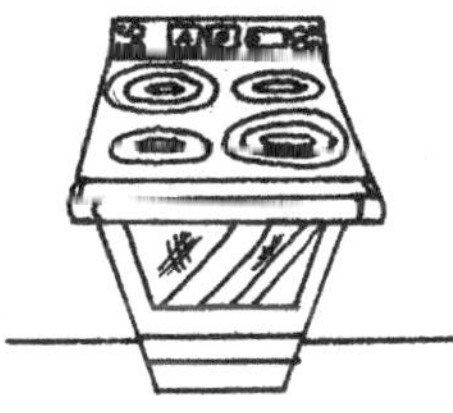
17) stovc

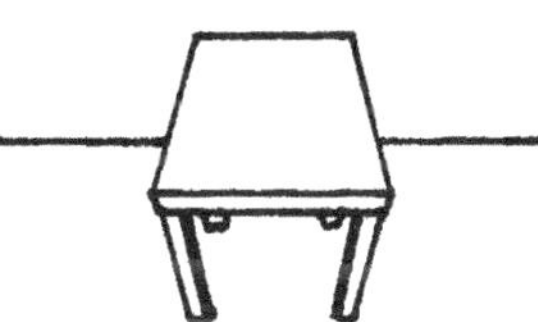
18) table

19) telephone

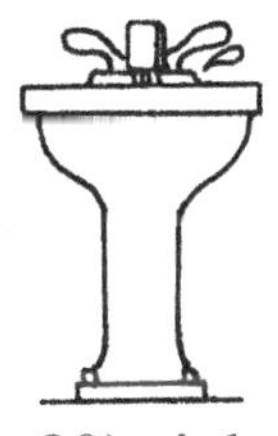
20) sink

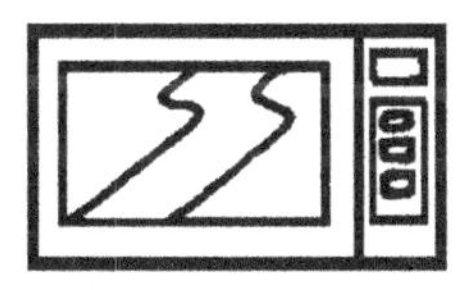
21) microwave

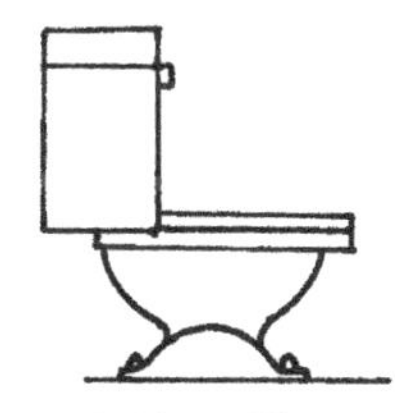
22) toilet

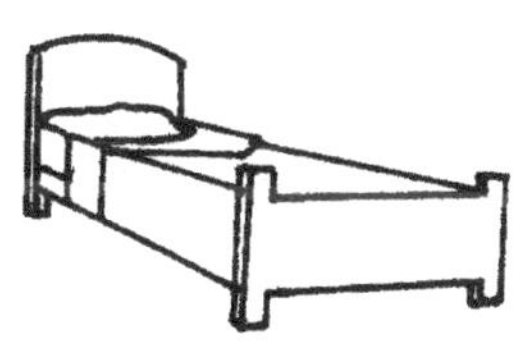
23) bed

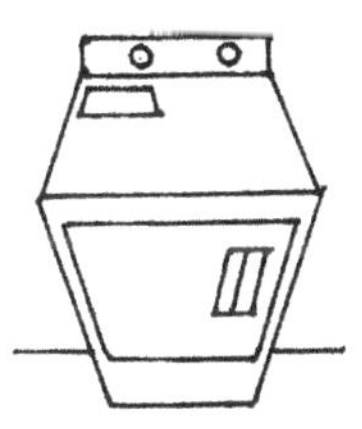
24) dryer

1-4

1) eomcprut

2) stesinul

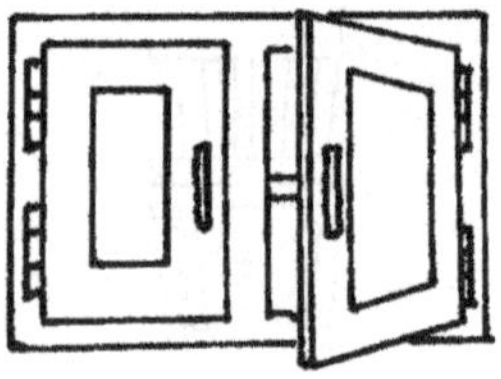

3) soucardbp

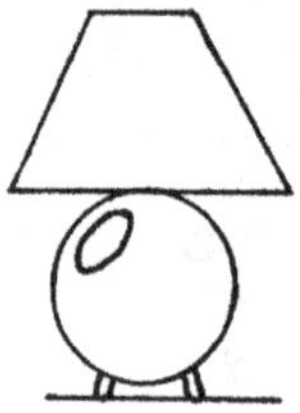

4) mapl

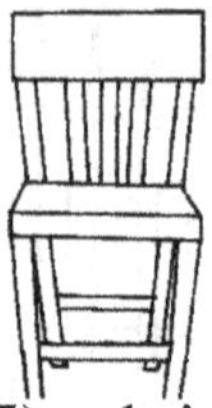

5) cahri

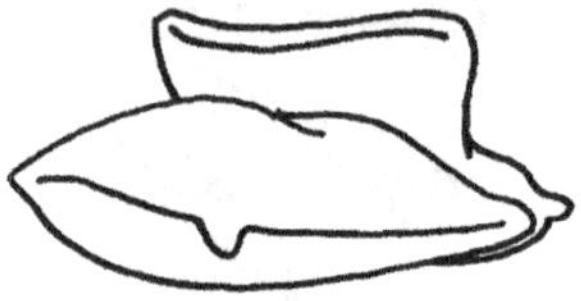

6) sliplow

7) rashwe

8) iilevtoens

9) raists

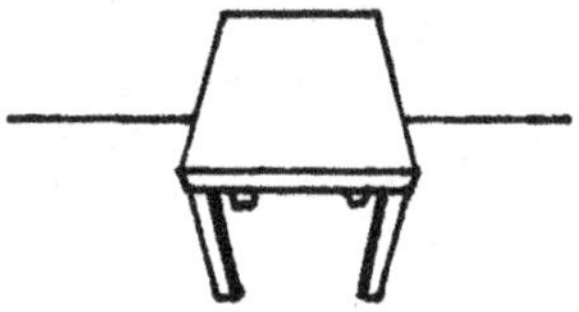

10) aeltb

11) kins

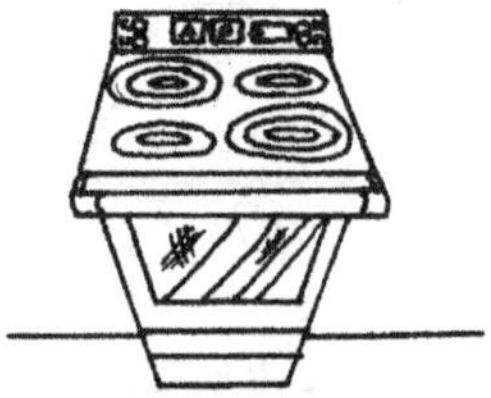

12) ovets

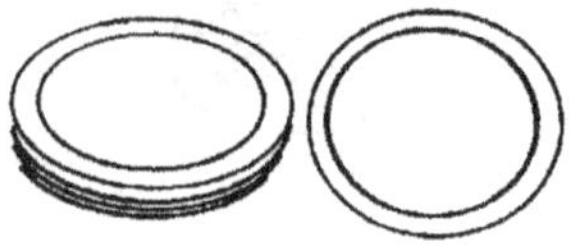

13) pealts

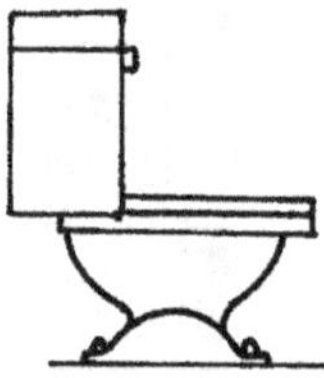

14) lioett

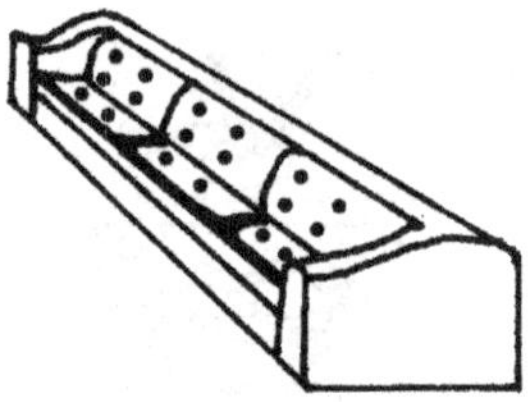

15) huocc

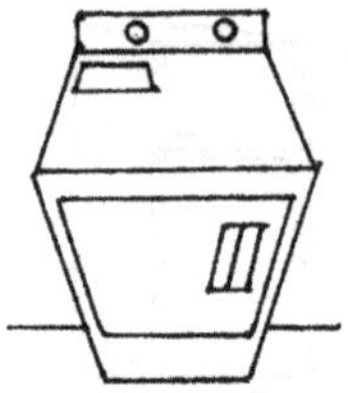

16) redyr

17) rvc

18) eerots

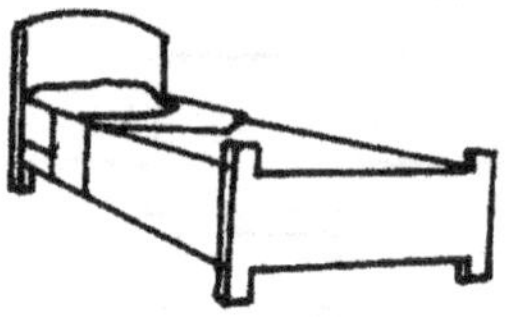

19) ebd

20) womeciavr

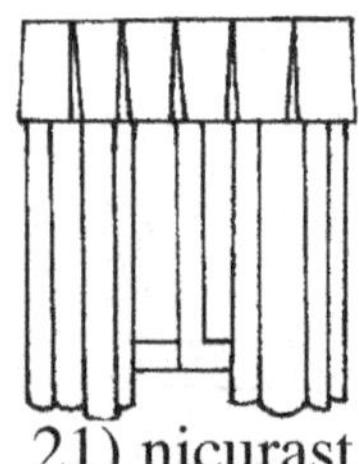

21) nicurast

22) phteeenol

23) grafrieroert

24) setloc

ORDERING

Put the words in alphabetical order.

vcr	stairs	computer	closet
lamp	curtains	table	refrigerator
toilet	pillows	couch	chair
bed	telephone	television	sink
stove	washer	stereo	plates
microwave	dryer	cupboards	utensils

1) _______________________

2) _______________________

3) _______________________

4) _______________________

5) _______________________

6) _______________________

7) _______________________

8) _______________________

9) _______________________

10) _______________________

11) _______________________

12) _______________________

13) _______________________

14) _______________________

15) _______________________

16) _______________________

17) _______________________

18) _______________________

19) _______________________

20) _______________________

21) _______________________

22) _______________________

23) _______________________

24) _______________________

QUIZ

1) List the items from this unit that require electricity to operate.

____

2) Using some of the letters in the word microwave, what other word from the list can you make?

____

3) List the words that end in a vowel.

____

DASHES

Complete each word by adding the missing letters. Each dash represents a letter.

1) t _ _ e _ _ _ _ e

2) t e _ e _ _ s _ _ n

3) w _ _ _ e r

4) l a _ _

5) s _ e _ e _

6) r _ _ r _ _ e _ _ t _ r

7) d _ _ _ r

8) c o _ _ u _ _ r

9) c _ a _ r

10) c _ _ c h

11) b _ d

12) c _ r _ _ i _ s

13) t _ _ l _ t

14) t _ _ l e

15) s _ _ v _

16) s _ _ k

17) s _ _ i r s

18) c _ _ _ o _ r _ s

19) c _ o _ e _

20) p l _ _ _ s

21) u _ e _ s _ l s

22) p _ _ l _ _ s

23) m _ _ _ _ w _ _ e

24) v _ r

WORD SPIRAL

Following the spiral towards the center, circle all the vocabulary words from this unit.

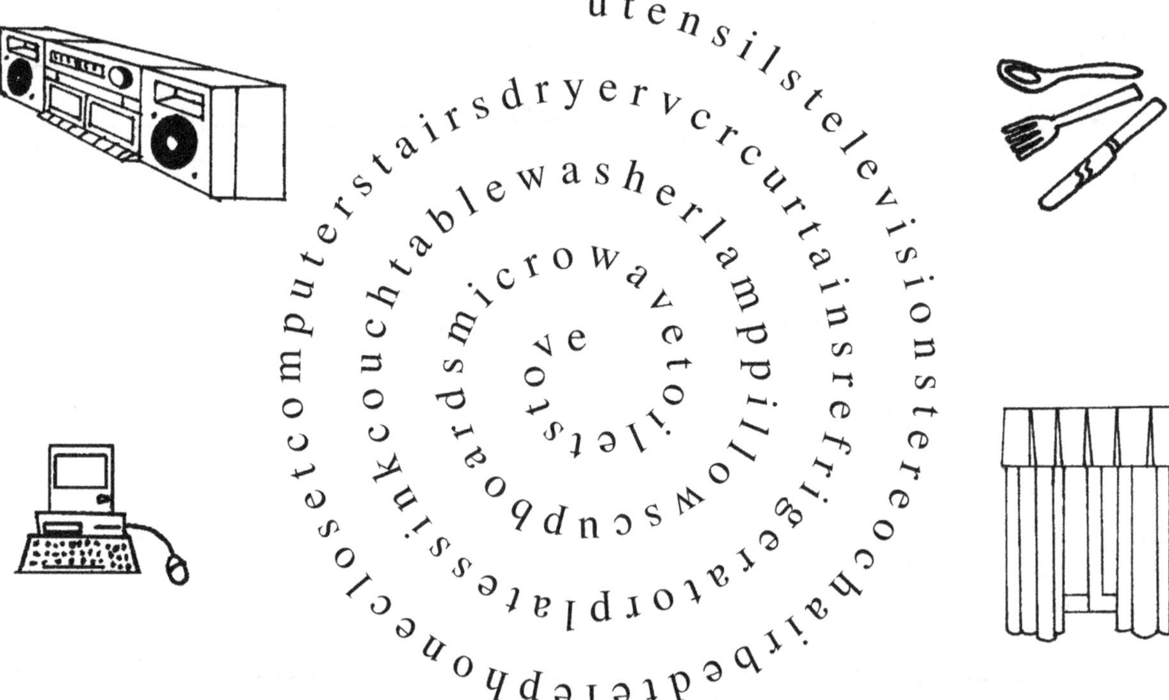

SCRAMBLES

Unscramble the jumbled letters to form words from this unit. Arrange the circled letters to form a surprise answer.

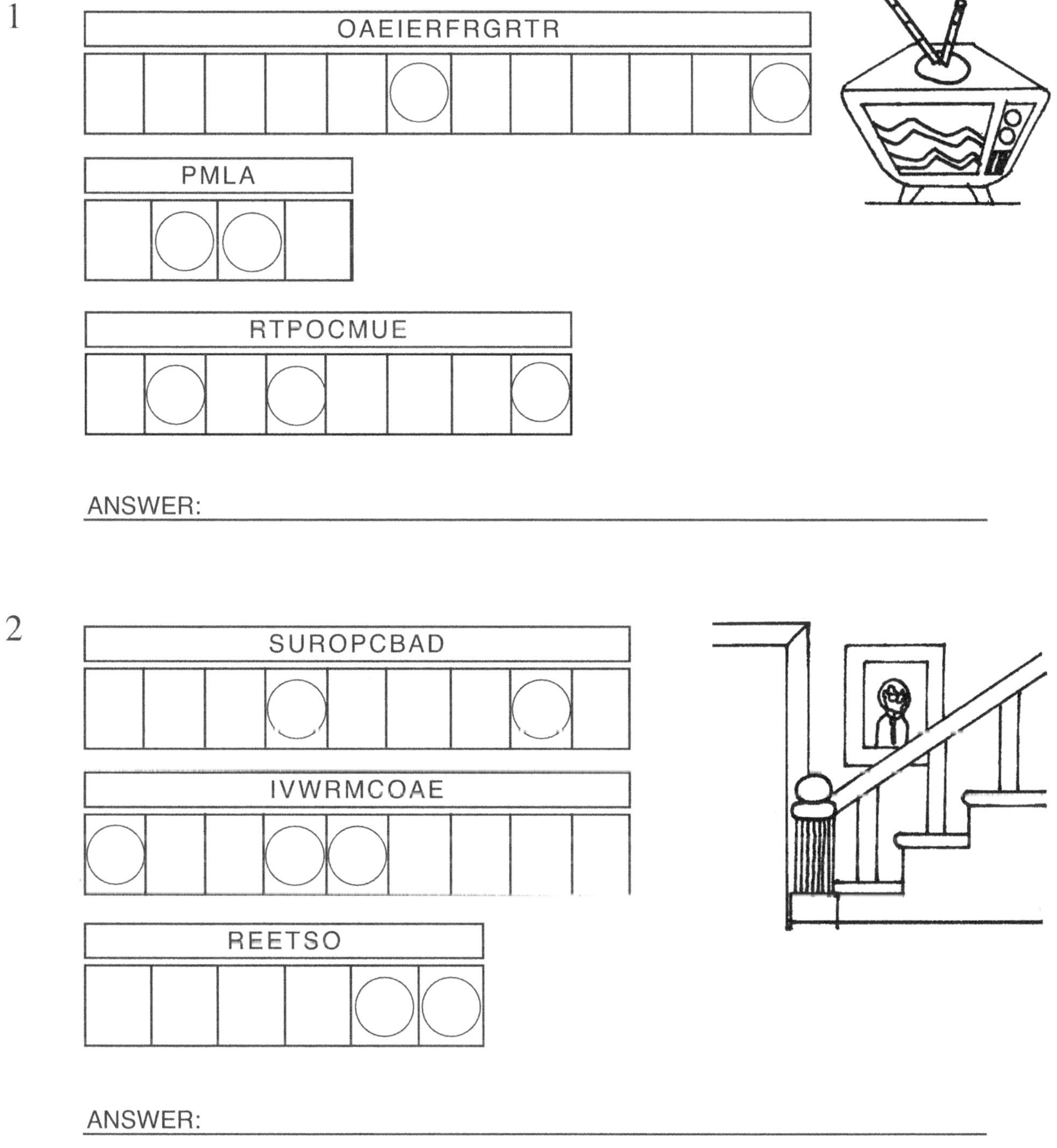

1

OAEIERFRGRTR

PMLA

RTPOCMUE

ANSWER: ____________________

2

SUROPCBAD

IVWRMCOAE

REETSO

ANSWER: ____________________

WORD MAZES

To find your way out of each maze, follow words from the unit from START to FINISH. The words can go from left-to-right, from right-to-left, upward, downward or diagonally.

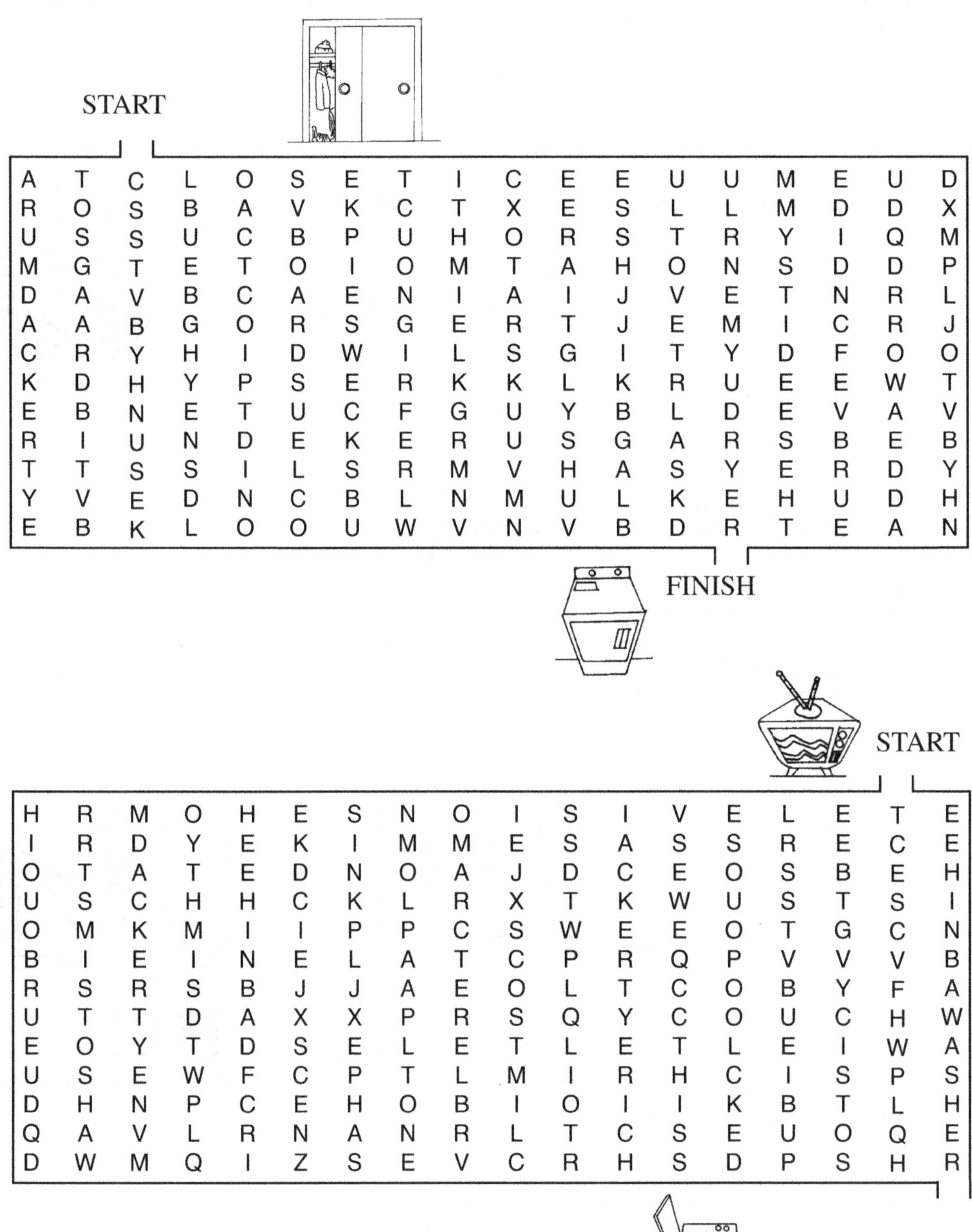

MAGIC WORD

Using words from the unit, complete the fill in the blanks exercise below. When you fill in those words on the chart an extra word will appear in the box.

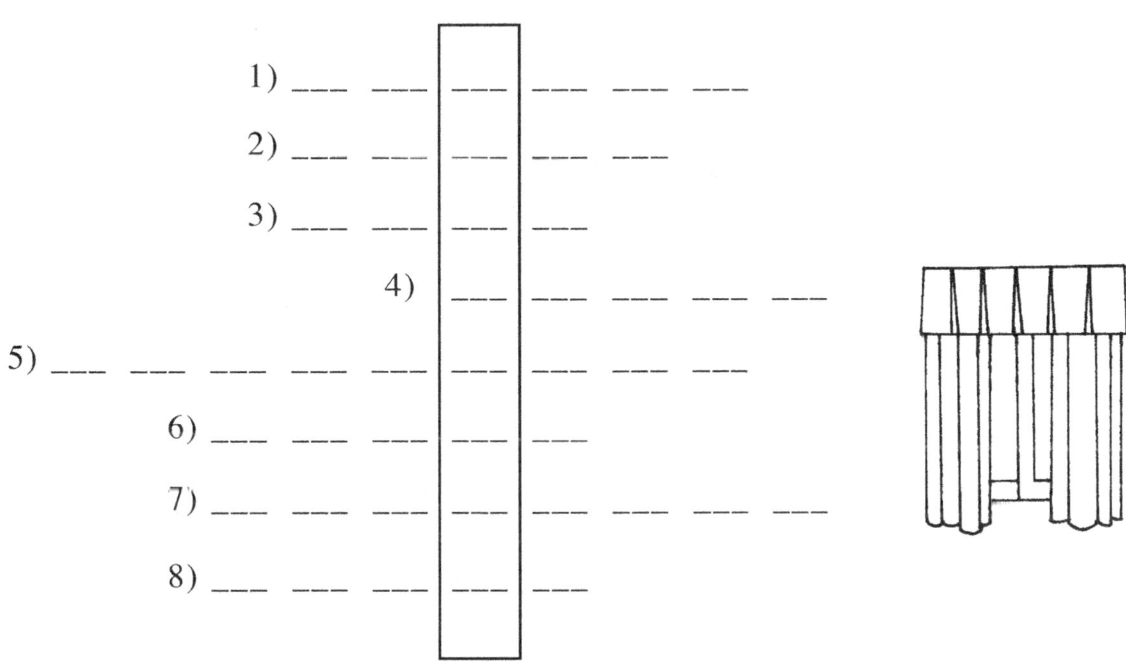

1) When clothes are dirty we put them in the _____________________.

2) My mother relaxes on the _____________________ after dinner.

3) Before I eat, I wash my hands at the _____________________.

4) Don't touch the _____________________ when it is hot.

5) My older sister is always talking on the _____________________.

6) The old man was tired, so he sat in a _____________________.

7) Forks, knives and spoons are types of _____________________.

8) Until we bought a _____________________, we used to hang our wet clothes on a line.

MAGIC WORD: _____________________

EIGHT MISTAKES

There are 8 things missing from Picture Two that can be found in Picture One. Find the
missing items and write them down.

1 ____

2 ____

3 ____

4 ____

5 ____

6 ____

7 ____

8 ____

CROSSWORD PUZZLE

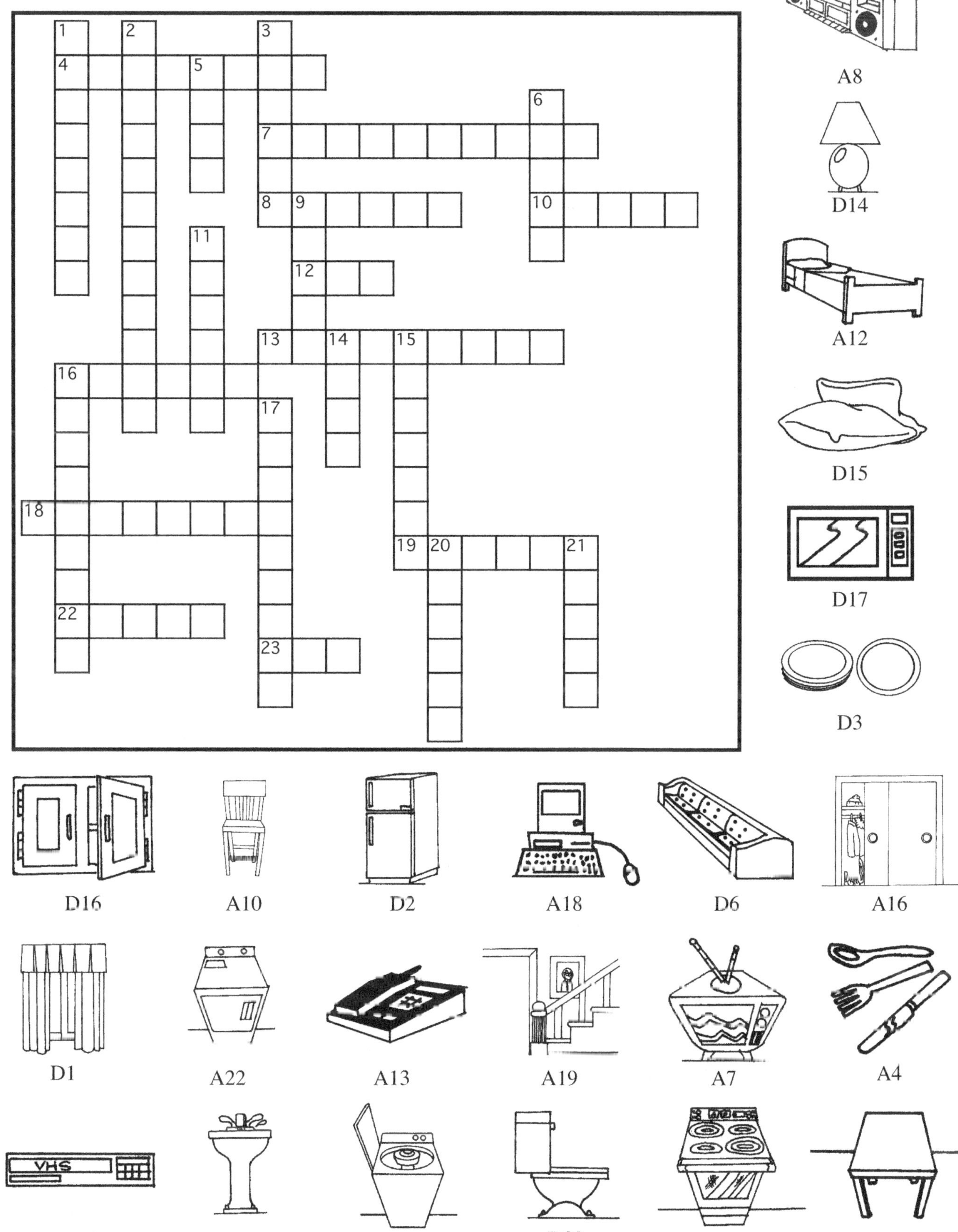

FIND-THE-WORDS PUZZLE

You will find all the words from this unit hidden in the box below. Find each word and circle all its letters. To find the words you may have to read from left-to-right, from right-to-left, upward, downward or diagonally.

```
R  E  F  R  I  G  E  R  A  T  O  R  W  R  O  O
E  V  J  W  P  Z  T  R  E  Y  R  D  O  E  S  T
H  A  K  E  O  W  O  H  V  M  B  M  N  T  L  V
S  W  O  L  L  I  P  E  Y  R  Y  X  D  U  I  D
A  O  L  N  C  E  M  S  A  E  I  N  E  P  S  V
W  R  M  A  H  C  A  T  W  T  T  A  R  M  N  O
A  C  I  E  E  C  L  O  S  E  T  A  H  O  E  E
B  I  J  X  A  R  S  V  U  M  E  R  F  C  T  R
H  M  D  E  Z  E  H  E  I  Y  L  E  S  L  U  E
C  E  C  U  R  T  A  I  N  S  E  I  T  L  T  T
U  F  Q  D  U  B  A  R  E  I  P  L  A  T  E  S
O  G  R  E  Y  N  D  T  W  N  H  L  I  I  L  P
C  U  P  B  O  A  R  D  S  K  O  O  R  F  I  O
C  H  S  T  U  X  O  Y  C  B  N  V  S  E  O  R
D  I  T  Y  Y  V  C  Y  N  A  E  L  B  A  T  C
T  E  L  E  V  I  S  I  O  N  Q  E  U  T  Z  V
```

BED	REFRIGERATOR
CHAIR	SINK
CLOSET	STAIRS
COMPUTER	STEREO
COUCH	STOVE
CUPBOARDS	TABLE
CURTAINS	TELEPHONE
DRYER	TELEVISION
LAMP	TOILET
MICROWAVE	UTENSILS
PILLOWS	VCR
PLATES	WASHER

1-13

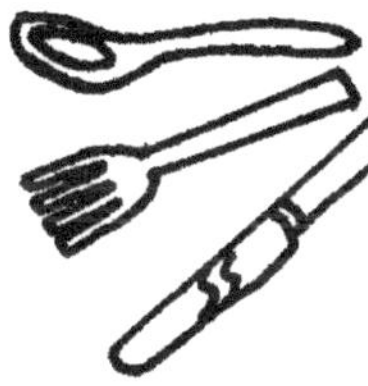

1)

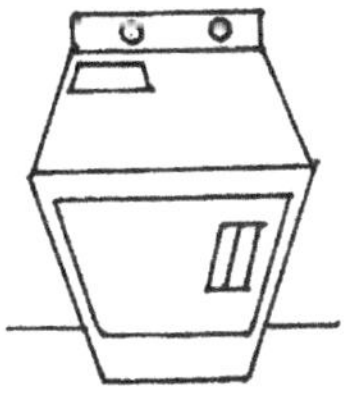

2)

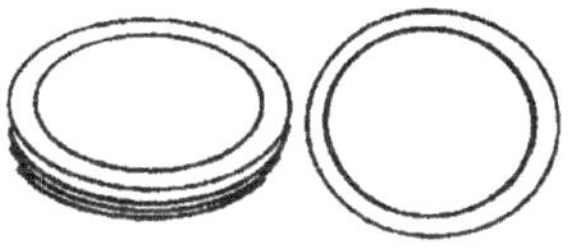

3)

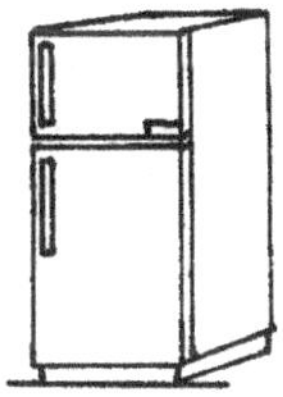

4)

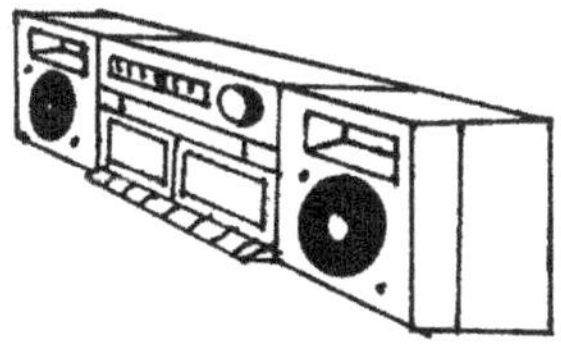

5)

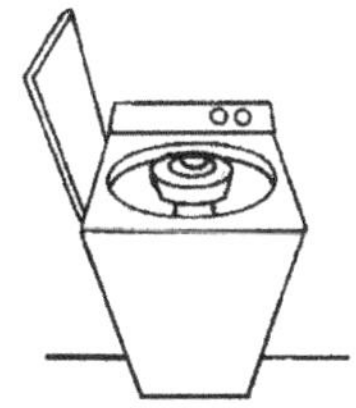

6)

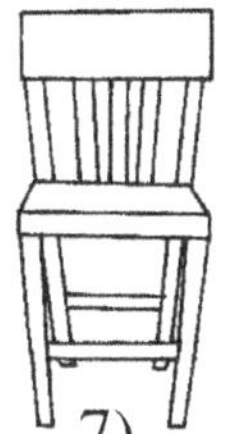

7)

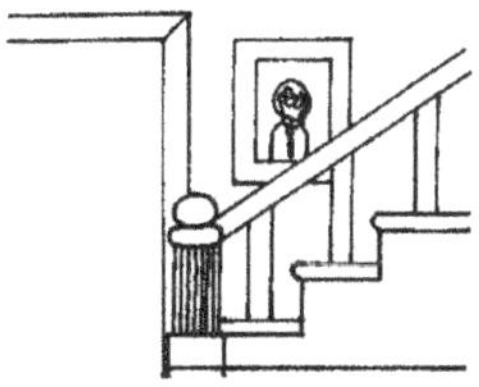

8)

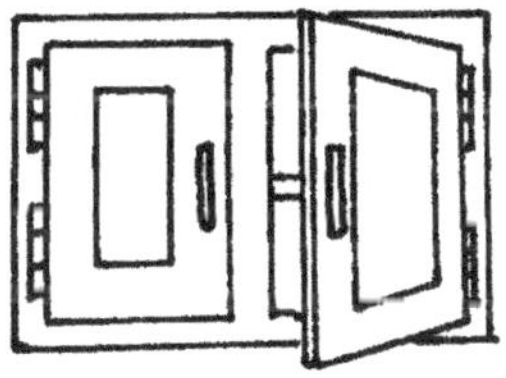

9)

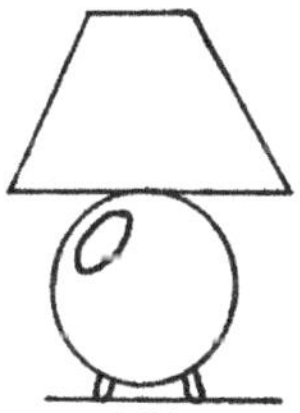

10)

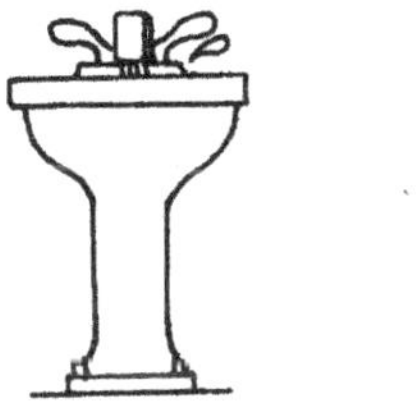

11)

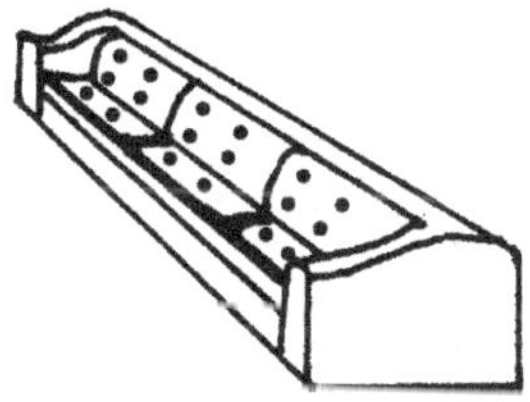

12)

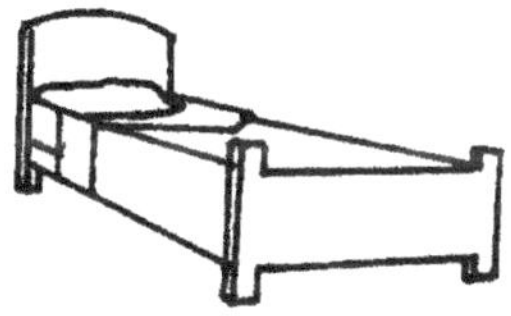

13)

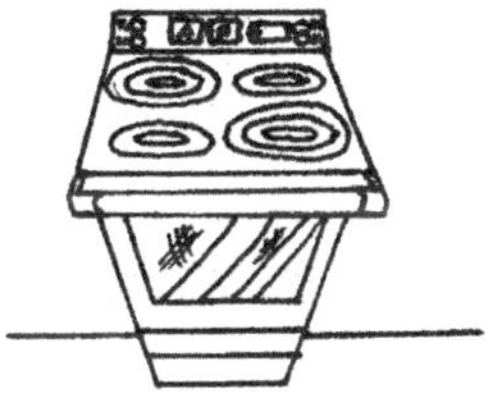

14)

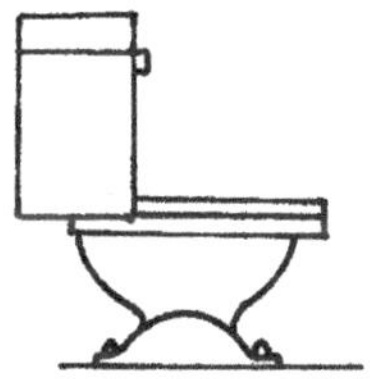

15)

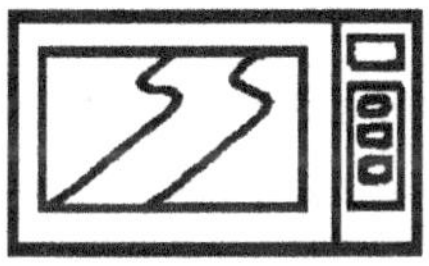

16)

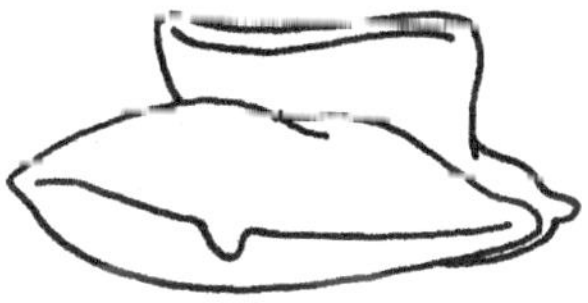

17)

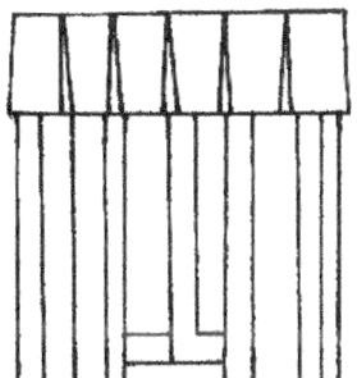

18)

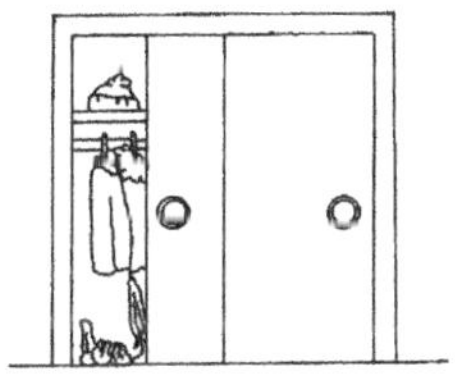

19)

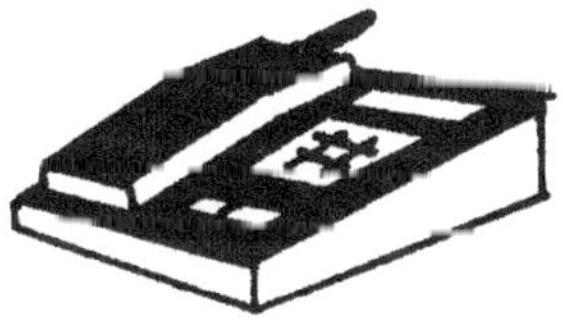

20)

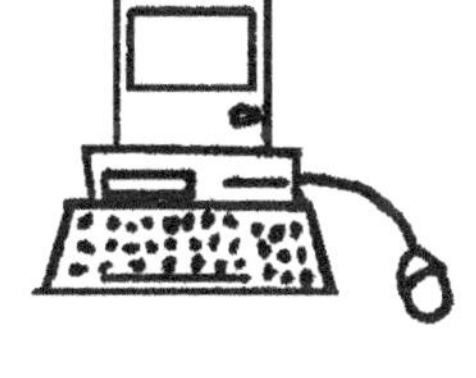

21)

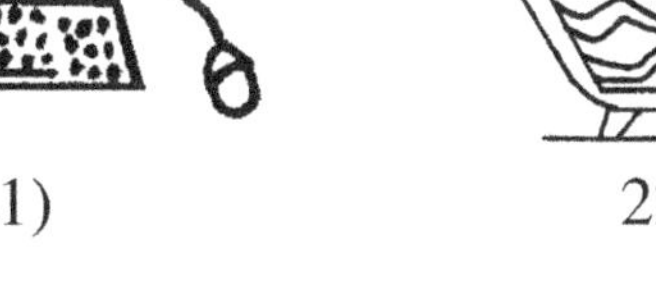

22)

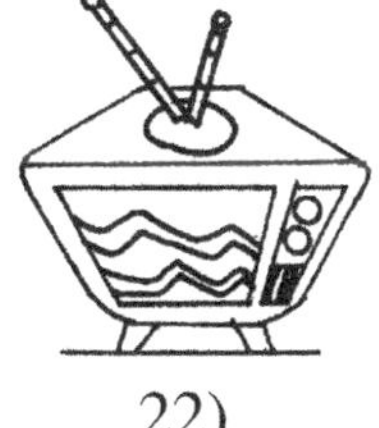

23)

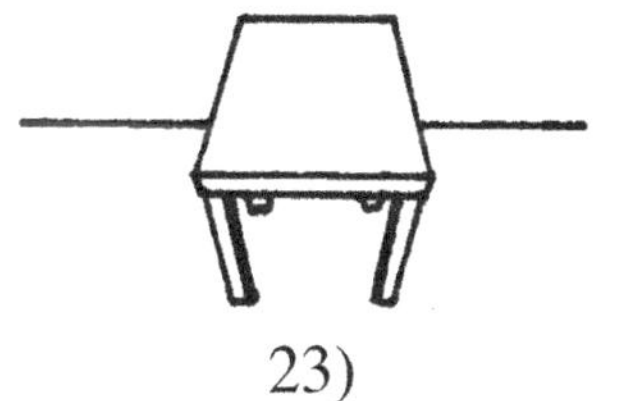

24)

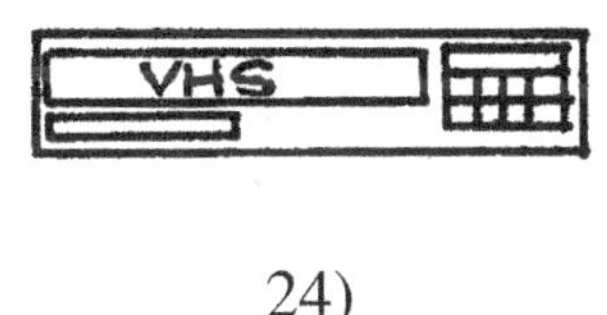

ANSWER KEY

DRAWINGS Page 4

1) computer 2) utensils 3) cupboards 4) lamp 5) chair 6) pillows 7) washer 8) television 9) stairs 10) table 11) sink 12) stove 13) plates 14) toilet 15) couch 16) dryer 17) vcr 18) stereo 19) bed 20) microwave 21) curtains 22) telephone 24) refrigerator 24) closet

ORDERING

1) bed 2) chair 3) closet 4) computer 5) couch 6) cupboards 7) curtains 8) dryer 9) lamp 10) microwave 11) pillows 12) plates 13) refrigerator 14) sink 15) stairs 16) stereo 17) stove 18) table 19) telephone 20) television 21) toilet 22) utensils 23) vcr 24) washer

QUIZ

1) television, washer, dryer, stereo, refrigerator, lamp, computer, stove, microwave, vcr

2) vcr

3) telephone, stereo, table, stove, microwave

DASHES

1) telephone 2) television 3) washer 4) lamp 5) stereo 6) refrigerator 7) dryer 8) computer 9) chair 10) couch 11) bed 12) curtains 13) toilet 14) table 15) stove 16) sink 17) stairs 18) cupboards 19) closet 20) plates 21) utensils 22) pillows 23) microwave 24) vcr

WORD SPIRAL

1) utensils 2) television 3) stereo 4) chair 5) bed 6) telephone 7) closet 8) computer 9) stairs 10) dryer 11) vcr 12) curtains 13) refrigerator 14) plates 15) sink 16) couch 17) table 18) washer 19) lamp 20) pillows 21) cupboards 22) microwave 23) toilet 24) stove

WORD MAZES

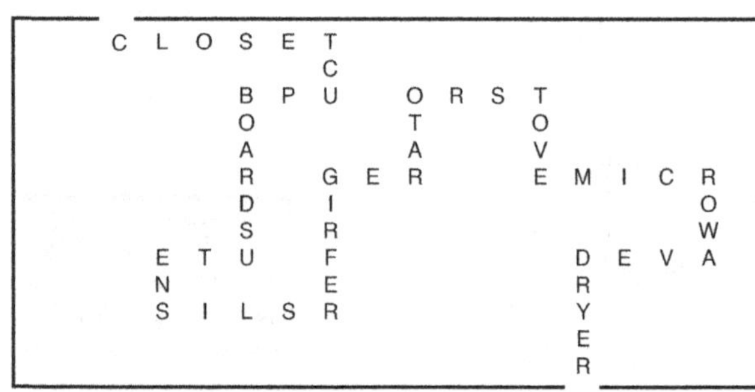

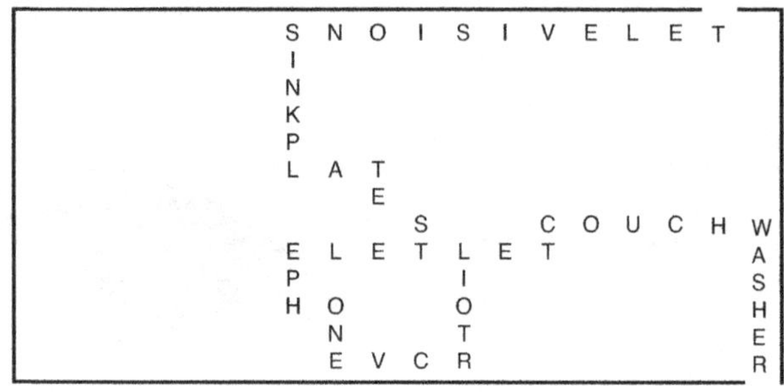

SCRAMBLES

1) program 2) bedroom

EIGHT MISTAKES

1) clock hand 2) tree from painting 3) cord from vcr
4) arm on coat tree 5) cat's collar 6) button on couch
7) 2nd pillow 8) marks on arm of rocking chair

FIND-THE-WORDS PUZZLE

MAGIC WORD

1) washer 2) couch 3) sink 4) stove 5) telephone 6) chair 7) utensils 8) dryer MAGIC WORD: sunshine

CROSSWORD PUZZLE

ACROSS: 4) utensils 7) television 8) stereo 10) chair 12) bed 13) telephone 16) closet 18) computer 19) stairs 22) dryer 23) vcr
DOWN: 1) curtains 2) refrigerator 3) plates 5) sink 6) couch 9) table 11) washer 14) lamp 15) pillows 16) cupboards
17) microwave 20) toilet 21) stove

TEST Page 13

1) utensils 2) dryer 3) plates 4) refrigerator 5) stereo 6) washer 7) chair 8) stairs 9) cupboards 10) lamp 11) sink 12) couch 13) bed 14) stove 15) toilet 16) microwave 17) pillows 18) curtains 19) closet 20) telephone 21) computer 22) television 23) table 24) vcr

Unit 2: Vehicles

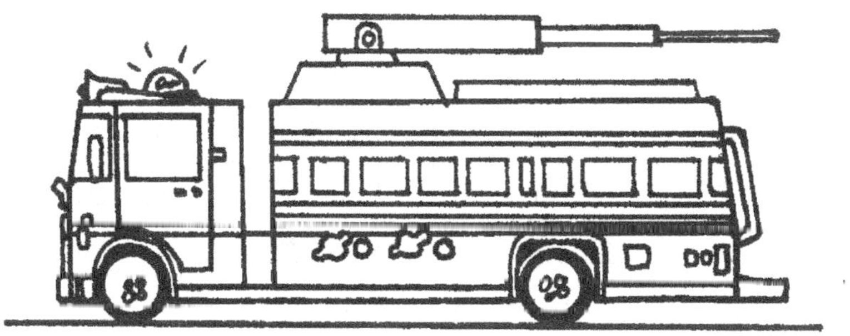

SENTENCES

1. The garbage truck takes our trash away once a week.
2. He is in the army and drives a tank.
3. The farmer used a tractor to plow the field.
4. I have a date on Saturday, so I will borrow my dad's car.
5. A dune buggy can drive on desert sand.
6. A snowmobile can travel on snow and ice.
7. An ambulance has a siren and flashing lights.
8. Gasoline is transported in a tanker truck.
9. The bulldozer pushed away the fallen old building.
10. The burglar was put in the police car.
11. My car broke down, so I called a tow truck.
12. She rides the bus to school.
13. A transport has eighteen wheels.
14. The jeep was great for summer driving.
15. When you ride a motorcycle, you should wear a helmet.
16. When I ordered soil for my garden, it came in a dump truck.
17. Our family outgrew our car, so we bought a van.
18. When you ride in a taxi, you have to pay a fare.
19. He used a backhoe to dig a hole.
20. They used a snowplow to clear the road after the blizzard.
21. The farmer uses a pickup truck to haul his vegetables to market.
22. The cement mixer poured concrete for the sidewalk.
23. A mobile home is a house on wheels.
24. There was a dalmatian riding on the fire engine.

1) garbage truck

2) tank

3) tractor

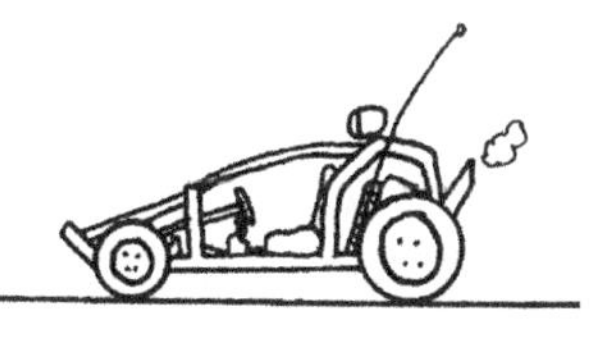

4) car

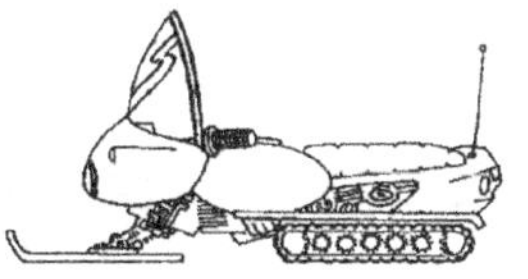

5) dune buggy

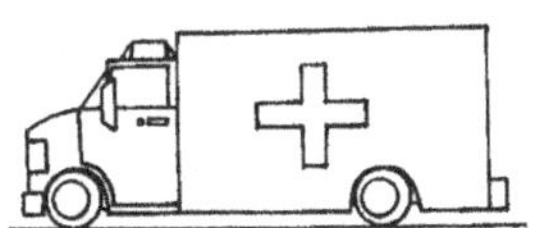

6) snowmobile

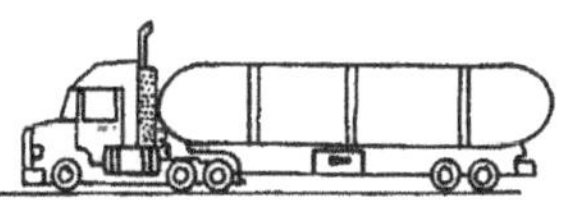

7) ambulance

8) tanker truck

9) bulldozer

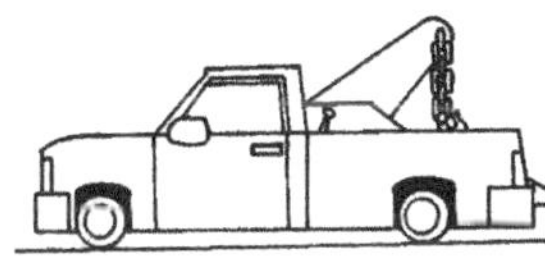

10) police car

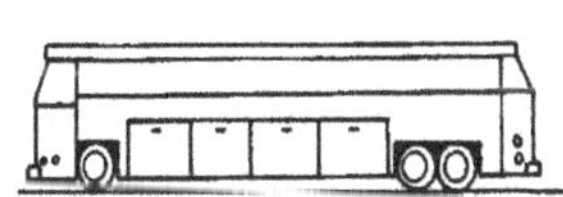

11) tow truck

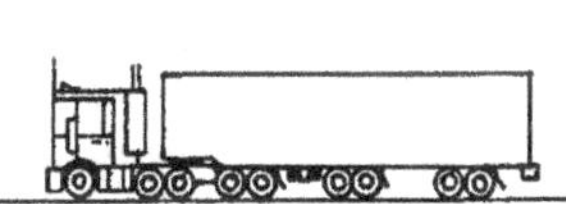

12) bus

13) transport

14) jeep

15) motorcycle

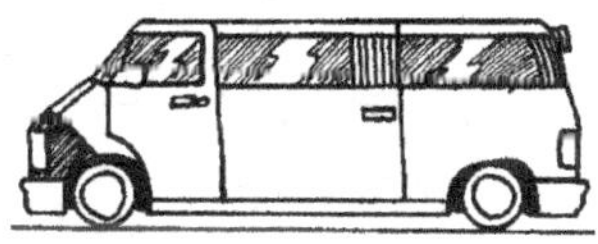

16) dump truck

17) van

18) taxi

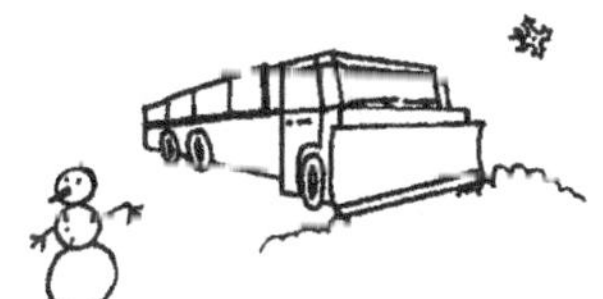

19) backhoe

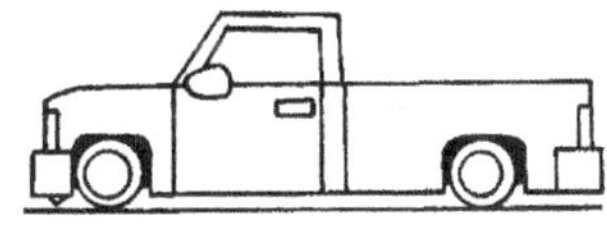

20) snowplow

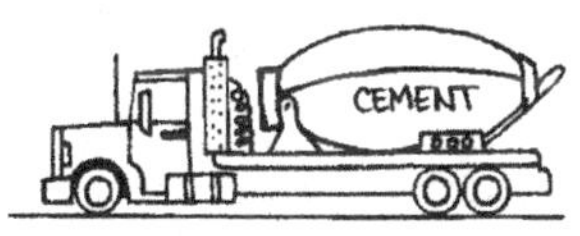

21) pickup truck

22) cement mixer

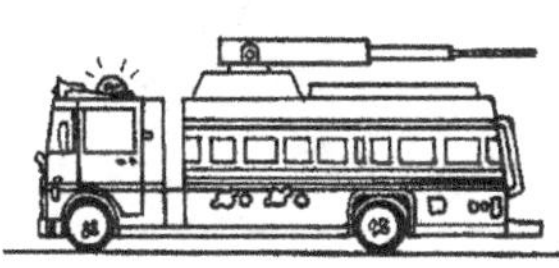

23) mobile home

24) fire engine

1) rottcar

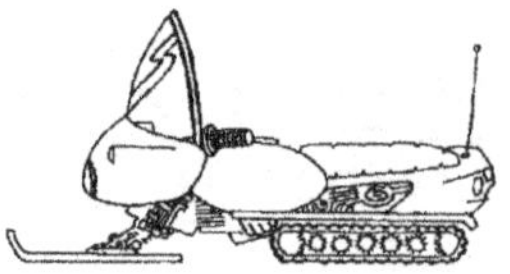

2) eslnoibwmo

3) locipe rac

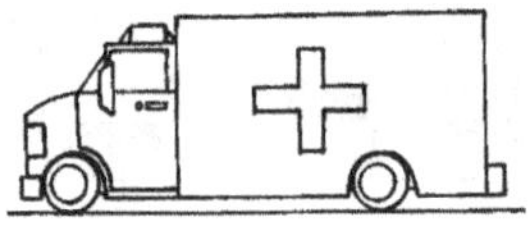

4) eacmnbalu

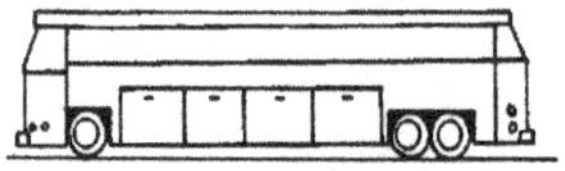

5) sub

6) roomtyccel

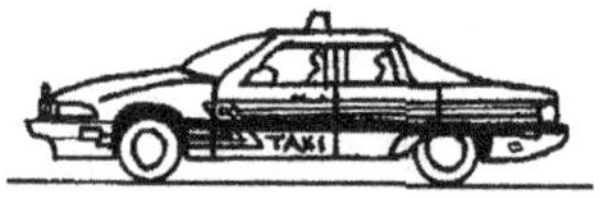

7) xait

8) egbagra crutk

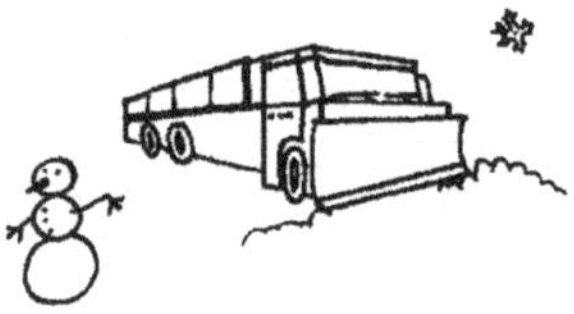

9) wowsnopl

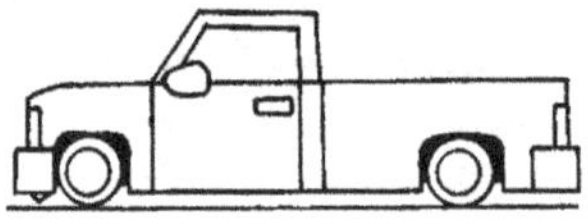

10) pupkic uctrk

11) kant

12) ratspront

13) enud gygbu

14) bomeli moeh

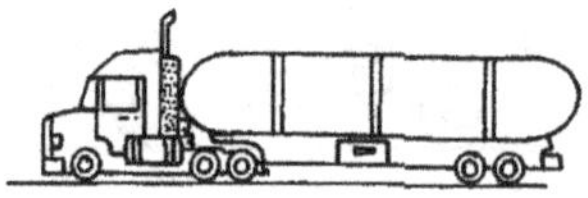

15) ketnar kctru

16) arc

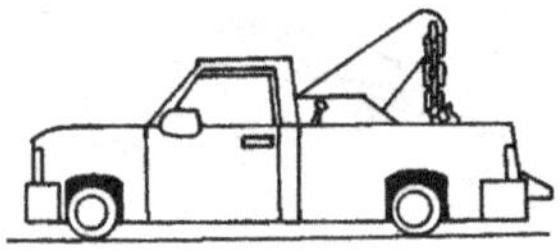

17) wto urckt

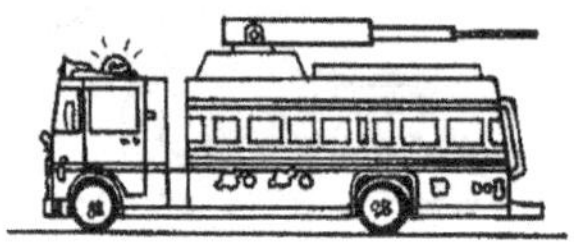

18) refi geenni

19) teemnc rexmi

20) zudllobre

21) mudp cturk

22) heabcok

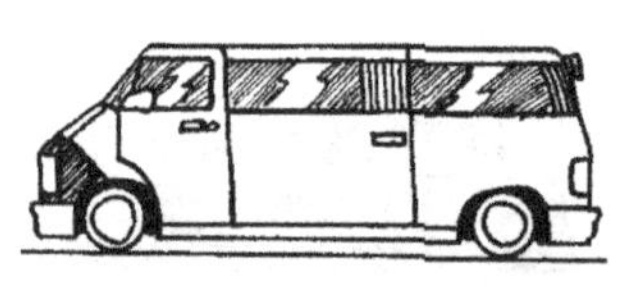

23) avn

24) epej

ORDERING

Put the words in alphabetical order.

backhoe	bus	bulldozer	motorcycle
police car	tow truck	van	fire engine
ambulance	tank	mobile home	jeep
taxi	tractor	garbage truck	dump truck
car	cement mixer	snowmobile	dune buggy
pickup truck	snowplow	transport	tanker truck

1) _______________________ 13) _______________________

2) _______________________ 14) _______________________

3) _______________________ 15) _______________________

4) _______________________ 16) _______________________

5) _______________________ 17) _______________________

6) _______________________ 18) _______________________

7) _______________________ 19) _______________________

8) _______________________ 20) _______________________

9) _______________________ 21) _______________________

10) _______________________ 22) _______________________

11) _______________________ 23) _______________________

12) _______________________ 24) _______________________

QUIZ

1) List the vehicles that are used for recreation.

____

2) List the vehicles that have a siren.

____

3) Which vehicles transport paying passengers?

____

DASHES

Complete each word by adding the missing letters. Each dash represents a letter.

1) p _ _ i _ e c _ r

2) c _ _ _ n t m _ _ _ r

3) d _ _ e b _ g _ _

4) s _ o _ p _ o w

5) m o _ _ _ c _ _ _ e

6) t _ _ k _ r t _ _ _ k

7) b _ l _ d _ _ _ r

8) t _ a _ s _ o _ t

9) b _ _

10) a _ b _ l _ n _ e

11) g _ _ b _ _ e t _ _ c _

12) j _ e _

13) m _ _ _ l e h _ _ e

14) s _ o _ m _ _ i _ e

15) p i _ _ _ p t _ u _ _

16) t _ w t _ u _ k

17) v _ _

18) f _ r _ e _ g _ n _

19) t _ _ i

20) c _ _

21) t a _ _

22) t r a _ _ _ r

23) b _ _ k h _ _

24) d _ _ p t _ _ _ k

WORD SPIRAL

Following the spiral towards the center, circle all the vocabulary words from this unit.

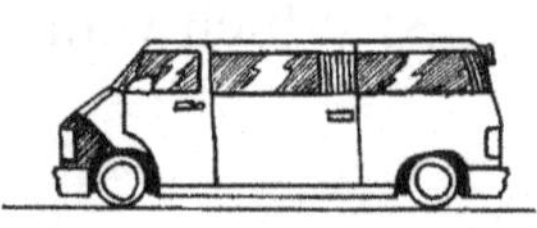

SCRAMBLES

Unscramble the jumbled letters to form words from this unit. Arrange the circled letters to form a surprise answer.

1

HEABCOK

AEACBULNM

MEECNT XREIM

ANSWER: ____

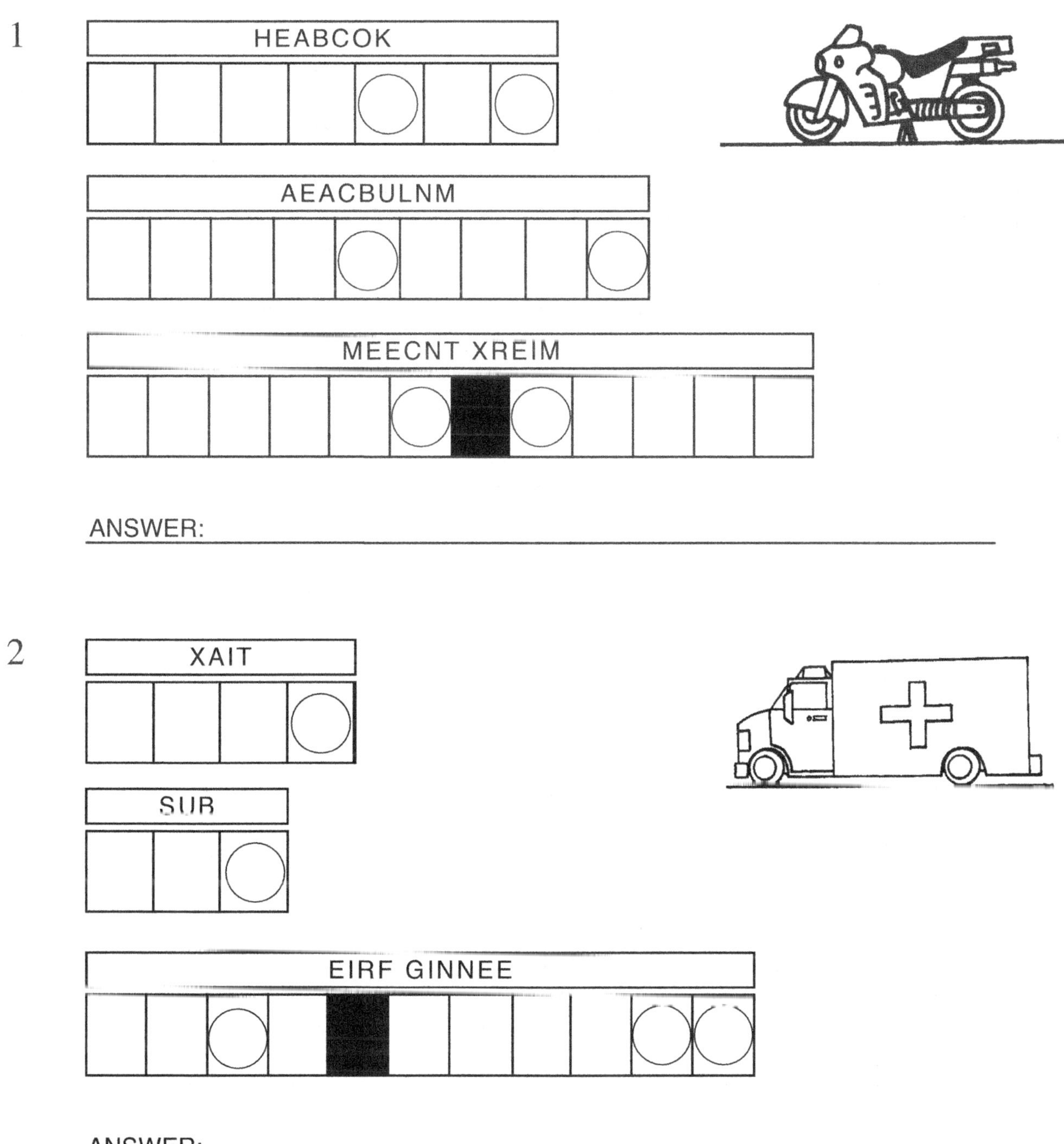

2

XAIT

SUB

EIRF GINNEE

ANSWER: ____

WORD MAZES

To find your way out of each maze, follow words from the unit from START to FINISH.
The words can go from left-to-right, from right-to-left, upward, downward or diagonally.

START

L	M	T	K	I	I	Z	L	H	R	I	Y	J	A	Z	N	V	T
D	P	A	L	U	A	X	I	I	C	R	U	A	L	C	J	H	P
I	L	N	S	O	O	E	N	N	T	P	C	N	S	B	I	G	U
O	J	K	A	Y	U	S	D	E	K	A	K	E	K	M	O	F	I
B	Z	G	S	H	E	A	G	S	R	N	A	H	D	N	K	R	F
R	S	P	A	G	S	A	T	O	I	I	M	B	U	L	A	Y	G
U	E	O	M	R	B	A	O	P	S	E	H	L	V	B	N	N	D
E	V	L	I	M	M	D	S	I	T	L	I	E	M	C	C	F	R
U	E	I	N	N	U	F	H	L	L	P	W	O	N	S	E	E	F
D	A	G	B	V	Q	G	A	O	D	L	D	V	E	P	W	L	H
Q	E	F	T	C	W	H	W	M	A	I	A	E	R	I	A	O	B
D	Y	E	R	X	E	J	B	A	N	L	G	L	T	Y	S	I	V
B	U	Q	E	D	R	J	A	C	K	H	O	E	Y	R	S	B	S

FINISH

START

M	T	P	S	R	F	E	M	O	H	E	L	I	B	O	M	T	M
B	Y	K	E	I	L	B	D	Y	E	K	W	P	R	J	O	P	P
G	Y	H	K	R	J	T	A	T	E	D	R	F	E	I	L	U	L
H	A	F	A	E	K	G	C	H	H	C	I	H	E	E	P	I	J
Y	S	S	C	E	H	V	K	M	I	I	T	U	J	N	D	F	Z
T	V	S	T	N	J	Y	E	I	N	E	S	V	R	R	U	G	S
U	G	T	C	G	B	N	R	S	B	J	F	E	E	I	N	D	S
R	T	V	O	D	I	S	T	D	A	X	E	S	Z	S	E	R	V
W	H	B	I	V	Q	N	Y	T	D	S	I	Y	O	F	B	F	E
E	I	Y	P	G	E	J	E	W	F	C	B	A	D	D	U	H	A
R	O	H	W	E	Z	A	N	P	C	E	U	L	L	X	G	B	E
R	P	N	E	R	X	N	V	L	R	N	P	A	S	P	G	V	Y
T	O	U	C	C	T	E	M	Q	I	Z	O	S	A	R	Y	S	U

FINISH

MAGIC WORD

Using words from the unit, complete the fill in the blanks exercise below. When you fill in those words on the chart an extra word will appear in the box.

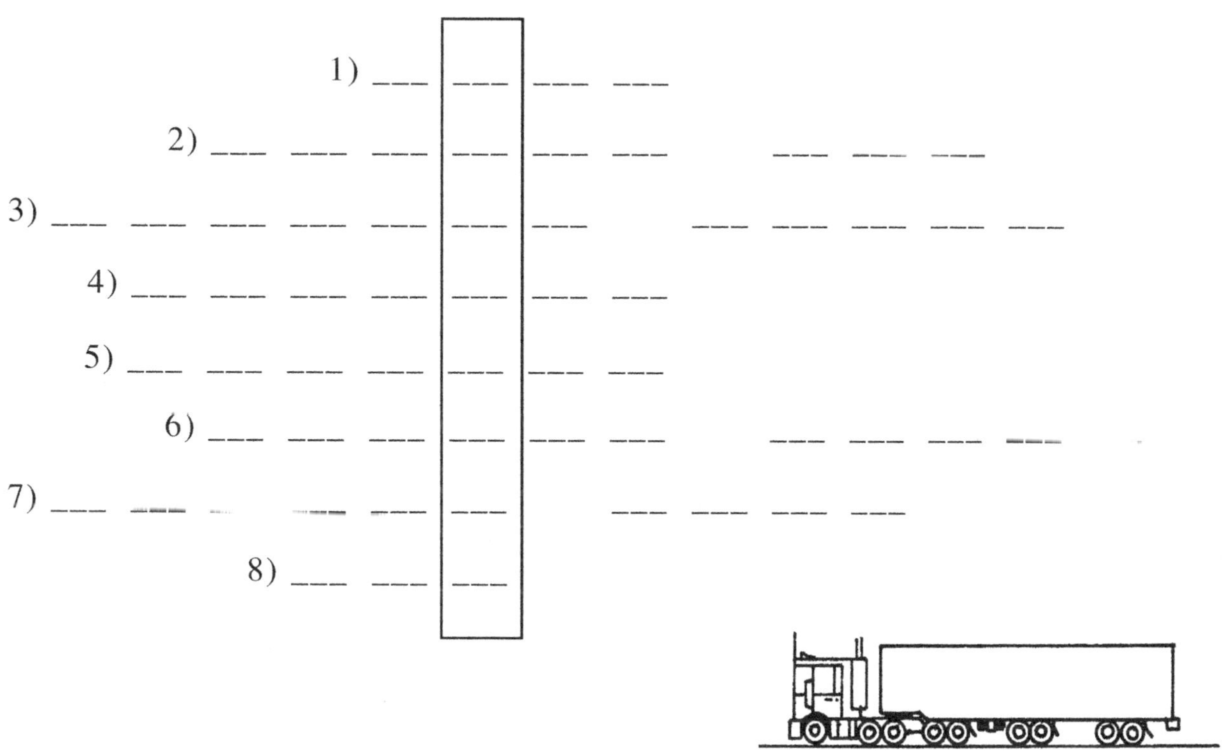

1) The _____________________ was great for summer driving.

2) The burglar was put in the _____________________.

3) The _____________________ takes our trash away once a week.

4) He used a _____________________ to dig a hole.

5) The farmer used a _____________________ to plow the field.

6) The _____________________ poured concrete for the sidewalk.

7) A _____________________ is a house on wheels.

8) Our family outgrew our car, so we bought a _____________________.

MAGIC WORD: _____________________

EIGHT MISTAKES

There are 8 things missing from Picture Two that can be found in Picture One. Find the missing items and write them down.

1 ____

2 ____

3 ____

4 ____

5 ____

6 ____

7 ____

8 ____

CROSSWORD PUZZLE

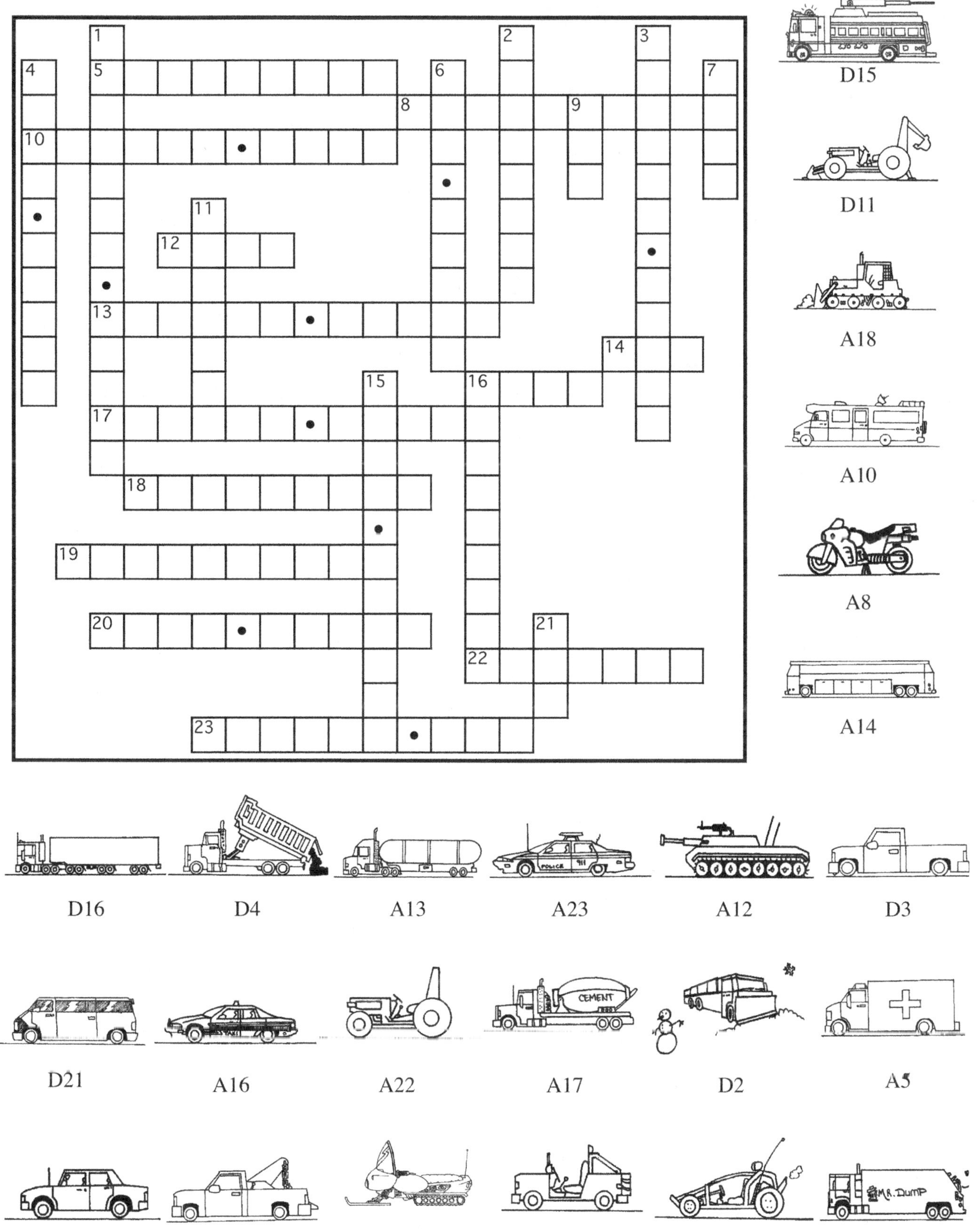

D15

D11

A18

A10

A8

A14

D16

D4

A13

A23

A12

D3

D21

A16

A22

A17

D2

A5

D9

D6

A19

D7

A20

D1

FIND-THE-WORDS PUZZLE

You will find all the words from this unit hidden in the box below. Find each word and circle all its letters. To find the words you may have to read from left-to-right, from right-to-left, upward, downward or diagonally.

```
A  B  T  H  M  T  A  N  K  E  R  T  R  U  C  K
M  L  O  R  E  X  I  M  T  N  E  M  E  C  G  Y
B  A  C  K  H  O  E  C  R  O  L  R  T  S  F  T
U  T  R  O  P  S  N  A  R  T  R  O  E  N  R  U
L  A  S  M  O  B  I  L  E  H  O  M  E  O  D  G
A  H  P  A  L  I  G  B  U  S  T  D  S  W  W  A
N  Y  I  D  I  E  N  A  J  E  E  P  T  M  O  R
C  R  C  O  C  A  E  Y  Q  L  R  S  E  O  L  B
E  E  K  C  E  M  E  G  T  C  I  K  W  B  P  A
U  Z  U  F  C  A  R  G  R  Y  C  C  A  I  W  G
R  O  P  E  A  A  I  U  A  C  R  U  E  L  O  E
V  D  T  R  R  X  F  B  C  R  D  R  R  E  N  T
G  L  R  T  A  E  L  E  T  O  O  T  T  Z  S  R
Y  L  U  T  A  F  I  N  O  T  C  W  H  A  O  U
U  U  C  Y  R  R  N  U  R  O  X  O  I  L  N  C
N  B  K  N  A  V  E  D  U  M  P  T  R  U  C  K
```

AMBULANCE	MOTORCYCLE
BACKHOE	PICKUP TRUCK
BULLDOZER	POLICE CAR
BUS	SNOWMOBILE
CAR	SNOWPLOW
CEMENT MIXER	TANK
DUMP TRUCK	TANKER TRUCK
DUNE BUGGY	TAXI
FIRE ENGINE	TOW TRUCK
GARBAGE TRUCK	TRACTOR
JEEP	TRANSPORT
MOBILE HOME	VAN

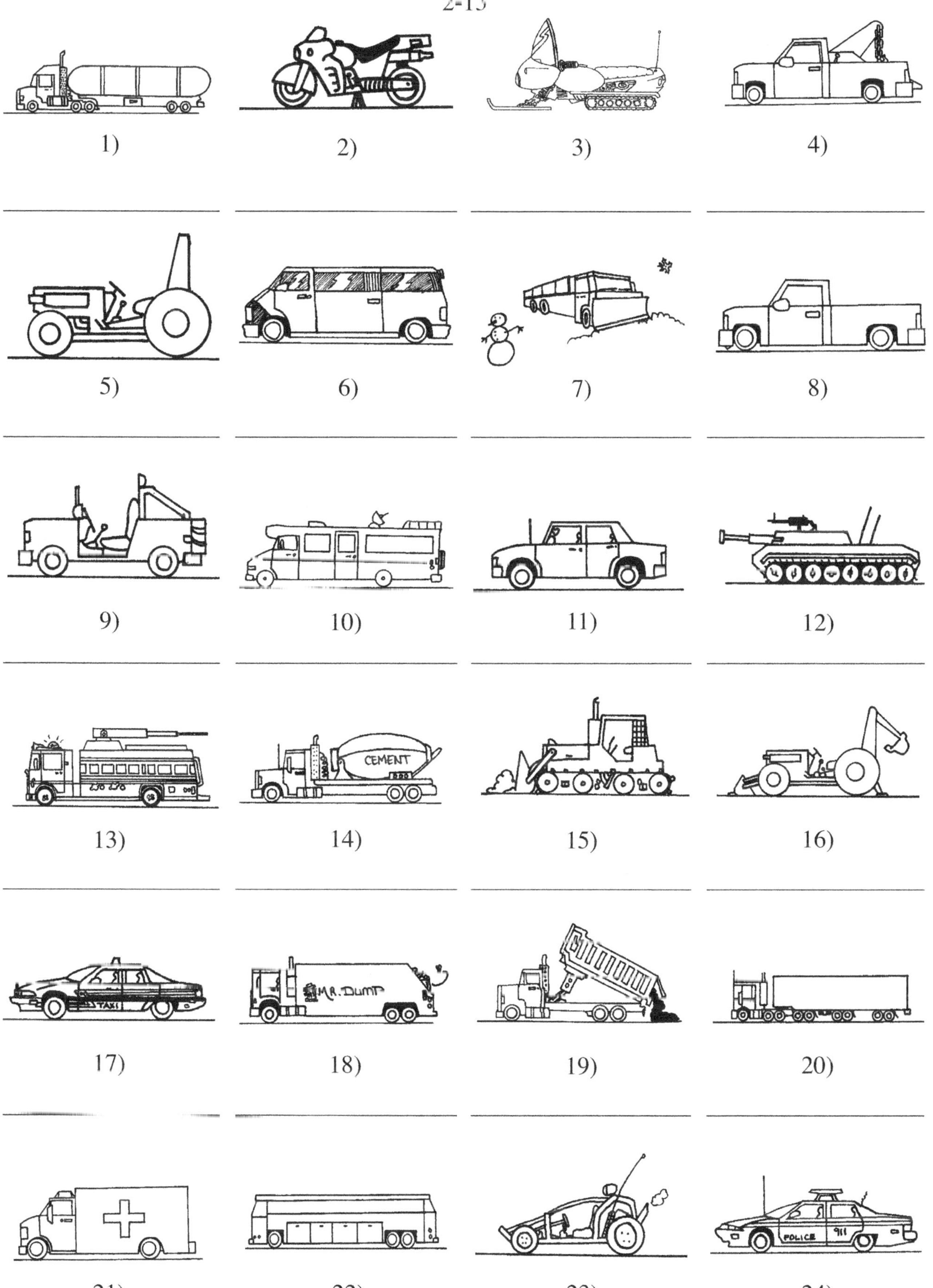

1)

2)

3)

4)

5)

6)

7)

8)

9)

10)

11)

12)

13)

14)

15)

16)

17)

18)

19)

20)

21)

22)

23)

24)

ANSWER KEY

DRAWINGS Page 4

1) tractor 2) snowmobile 3) police car 4) ambulance 5) bus 6) motorcycle 7) taxi 8) garbage truck 9) snowplow 10) pickup truck 11) tank 12) transport 13) dune buggy 14) mobile home 15) tanker truck 16) car 17) tow truck 18) fire engine 19) cement mixer 20) bulldozer 21) dump truck 22) backhoe 23) van 24) jeep

ORDERING

1) ambulance 2) backhoe 3) bulldozer 4) bus 5) car 6) cement mixer 7) dump truck 8) dune buggy 9) fire engine 10) garbage truck 11) jeep 12) mobile home 13) motorcycle 14) pickup truck 15) police car 16) snowmobile 17) snow plow 18) tank 19) tanker truck 20) taxi 21) tow truck 22) tractor 23) transport 24) van

QUIZ

1) mobile home, snowmobile, dune buggy
2) police car, ambulance, fire engine
3) taxi, bus, ambulance?

DASHES

1) police car 2) cement mixer 3) dune buggy 4) snowplow 5) motorcycle 6) tanker truck 7) bulldozer 8) transport 9) bus 10) ambulance 11) garbage truck 12) jeep 13) mobile home 14) snowmobile 15) pickup truck 16) tow truck 17) van 18) fire engine 19) taxi 20) car 21) tank 22) tractor 23) backhoe 24) dump truck

WORD SPIRAL

1) tanker truck 2) motorcycle 3) snowmobile 4) tow truck 5) tractor 6) van 7) snowplow 8) pickup truck 9) jeep 10) mobile home 11) car 12) tank 13) fire engine 14) cement mixer 15) bulldozer 16) backhoe 17) taxi 18) garbage truck 19) dump truck 20) transport 21) ambulance 22) bus 23) dune buggy 24) police car

WORD MAZES

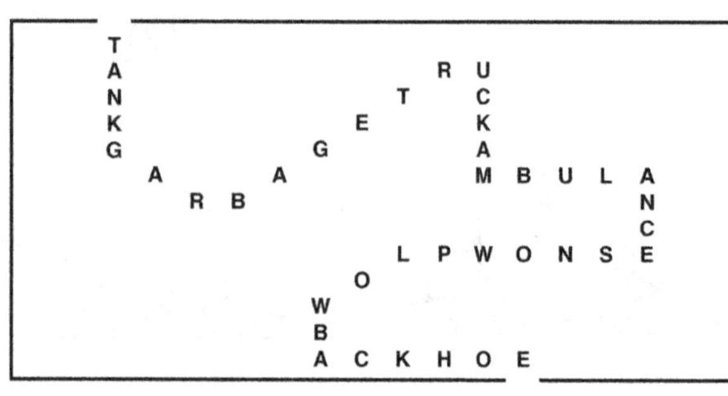

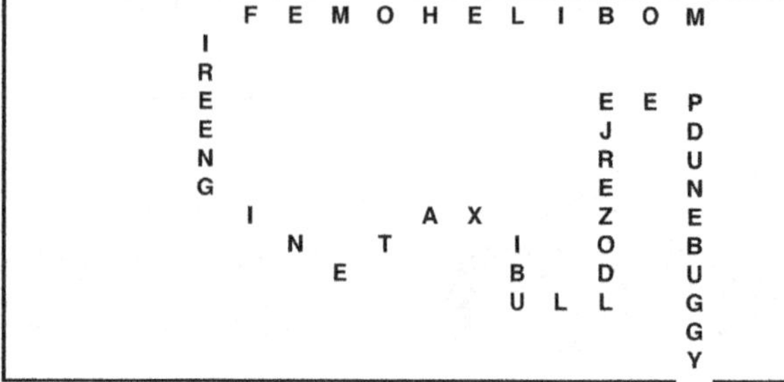

SCRAMBLES

1) helmet 2) siren

EIGHT MISTAKES

1) middle bird on ground 2) stripes on airplane wings 3) 911 missing from ambulance 4) leg of horse on the left 5) moose 6) driver of van missing 7) sun 8) person and motorcycle

FIND-THE-WORDS PUZZLE

A				T	A	N	K	E	R		T	R	U	C	K
M			R	E	X	I	M	T	N	E	M	E	C		
B	A	C	K	H	O	E						S			
U	T	R	O	P	S	N	A	R	T			N			
L		M	O	B	I	L	E	H	O	M	E	O			G
A		P		L		G	B	U	S			W	W		A
N		I		L		N		J	E	E	P	M	O		R
C	R	C		C		E	Y		L			O	L		B
E	E	K		E		E	G	T	C		K	B	P		A
	Z	U		C	A	R	G	R	Y		C	I	W		G
	O	P		A		I	U	A	C		U	L	O		E
	D	T		R	X	F	B	C	R		R	E	N		T
	L	R		A		E	T	O		T	T	S			R
	L	U	T			N	O	T		W		A			U
	U	C				U	R	O		O			N		C
	B	K	N	A	V		D	U	M	P	T	R	U	C	K

MAGIC WORD

1) jeep 2) police car 3) garbage truck 4) backhoe 5) tractor 6) cement mixer 7) mobile home 8) van MAGIC WORD: eighteen

CROSSWORD PUZZLE

ACROSS: 5) ambulance 8) motorcycle 10) mobile home 12) tank 13) tanker truck 14) bus 16) taxi 17) cement mixer 18) bulldozer 19) snowmobile 20) dune buggy 22) tractor 23) police car DOWN: 1) garbage truck 2) snowplow 3) pickup truck 4) dump truck 6) tow truck 7) jeep 9) car 11) backhoe 15) fire engine 16) transport 21) van

TEST Page 13

1) tanker truck 2) motorcycle 3) snowmobile 4) tow truck 5) tractor 6) van 7) snowplow 8) pickup truck 9) jeep 10) mobile home 11) car 12) tank 13) fire engine 14) cement mixer 15) bulldozer 16) backhoe 17) taxi 18) garbage truck 19) dump truck 20) transport 21) ambulance 22) bus 23) dune buggy 24) police car

Unit 3: Food

SENTENCES

1. He put some chops on the barbecue.
2. I eat chicken noodle soup whenever I am sick.
3. Fish can be fried, baked or broiled.
4. My favorite type of cheese is cheddar.
5. They usually eat a roast on Sunday.
6. Bacon comes from pigs.
7. Pasta with tomato sauce is my favorite meal.
8. I love the smell of freshly baked cookies.
9. My mom likes her eggs scrambled.
10. Milk helps to make your bones strong.
11. Rice is a popular side dish.
12. I think chicken tastes best when it is cooked on a grill.
13. The prisoner was fed bread and water.
14. I prefer my steak rare.
15. Beans are a good source of protein.
16. He ate a ham sandwich with mustard for lunch.
17. Apples and oranges are fruits.
18. Broccoli and carrots are types of vegetables.
19. Crackers are a nice snack.
20. Freshly squeezed orange juice is great for breakfast.
21. Some kinds of pickles are sour.
22. Cereal is a common breakfast food.
23. Whenever I eat seafood, I wear a bib.
24. She likes butter on her popcorn.

1) chops

2) soup

3) fish

4) cheese

5) roast

6) bacon

7) pasta

8) cookies

9) eggs

10) milk

11) rice

12) chicken

13) bread

14) steak

15) beans

16) ham

17) fruits

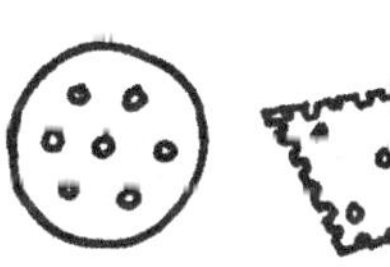

18) vegetables

19) crackers

20) juice

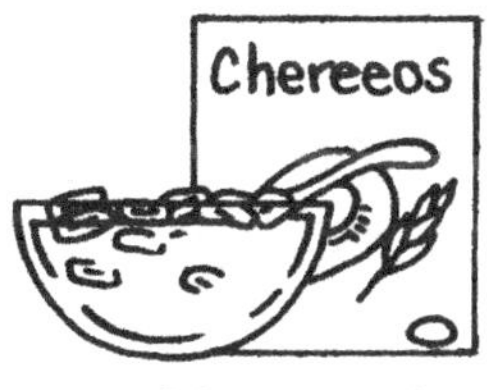

21) pickles

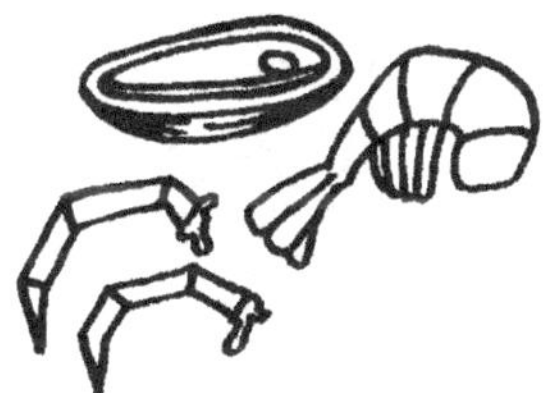

22) cereal

23) seafood

24) butter

1) puso

2) likm

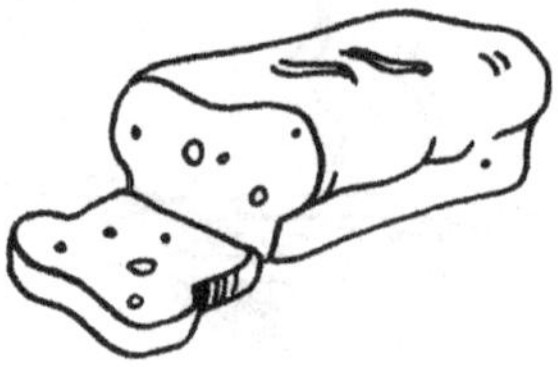

3) dearb

4) tasap

5) nicheck

6) cejiu

7) eehesc

8) mah

9) retbut

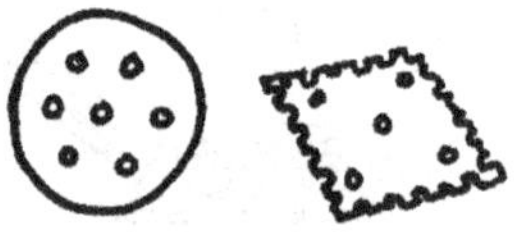

10) creaskcr

11) learce

12) shocp

13) noacb

14) shif

15) stufri

16) sneab

17) bleegveats

18) kiocose

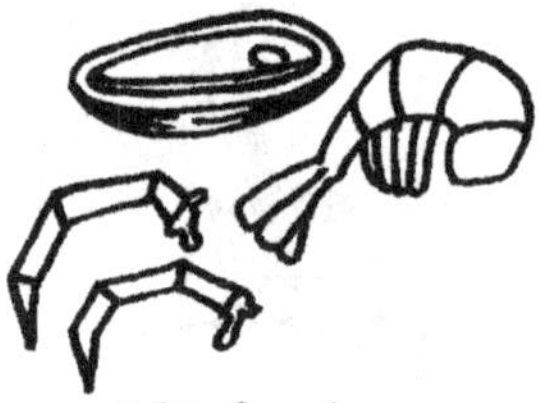

19) feadsoo

20) strao

21) eric

22) lipseck

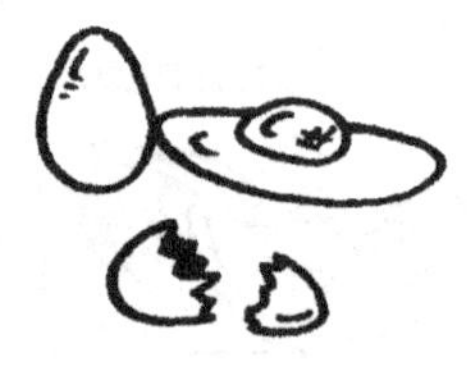

23) gegs

24) teaks

ORDERING

Put the words in alphabetical order.

beans	juice	ham	vegetables
pasta	cheese	roast	pickles
steak	soup	chops	cookies
bread	fish	rice	cereal
chicken	eggs	seafood	butter
milk	bacon	fruits	crackers

1) ________________________   13) ________________________

2) ________________________   14) ________________________

3) ________________________   15) ________________________

4) ________________________   16) ________________________

5) ________________________   17) ________________________

6) ________________________   18) ________________________

7) ________________________   19) ________________________

8) ________________________   20) ________________________

9) ________________________   21) ________________________

10) ________________________   22) ________________________

11) ________________________   23) ________________________

12) ________________________   24) ________________________

QUIZ

1) List the foods that come from the ocean.

____

2) List the words that have 2 consecutive vowels.

____

3) Pretend that you own a restaurant. Using the words in the list, create a menu.

____

DASHES

Complete each word by adding the missing letters. Each dash represents a letter.

1) c _ _ c _ _ n
2) s _ _ _
3) b _ a _ s
4) r _ a _ t
5) f _ _ i _ s
6) c _ _ e _ l
7) f _ _ h
8) b _ _ o _
9) j _ _ c _
10) s t _ _ _
11) c _ e _ _ e
12) b _ _ _ d

13) h _ _
14) s e _ _ o _ d
15) c o _ _ i _ s
16) c _ _ _ s
17) b _ _ t _ _
18) v _ _ e _ _ b _ _ s
19) r _ _ e
20) p i _ _ l _ s
21) c _ a _ k _ r _
22) m _ l _
23) e _ _ s
24) p _ s _ a

WORD SPIRAL

Following the spiral towards the center, circle all the vocabulary words from this unit.

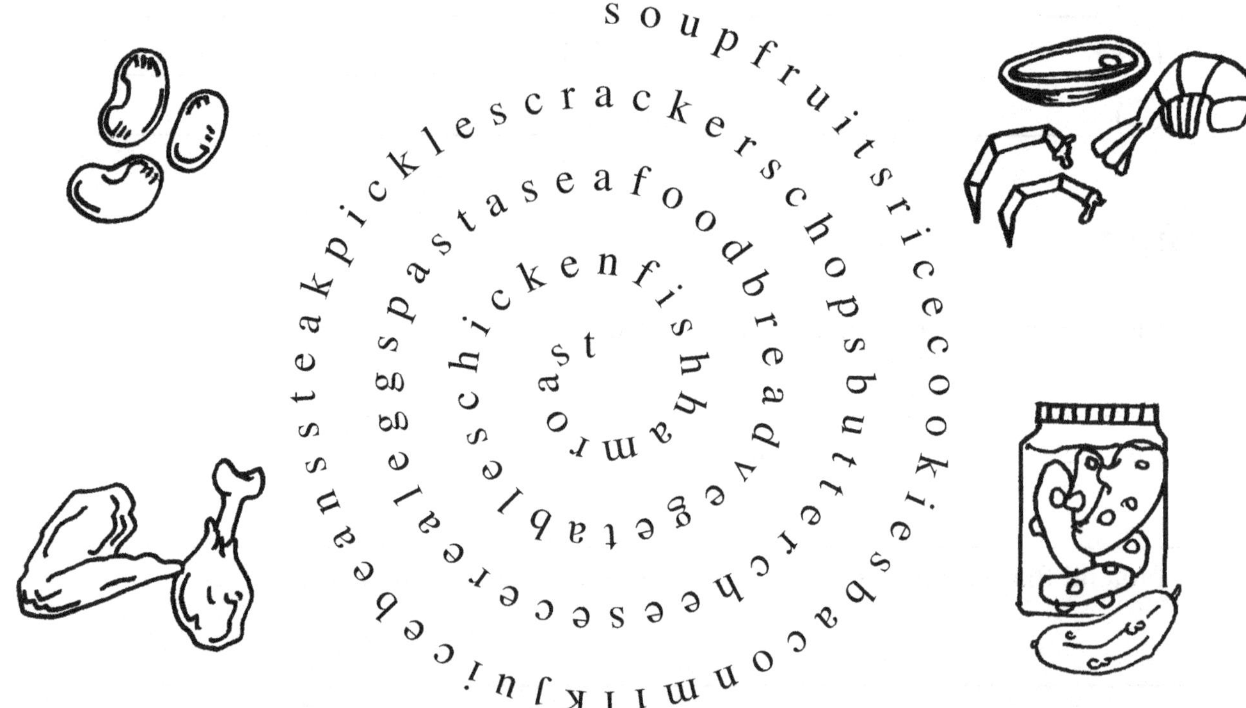

SCRAMBLES

Unscramble the jumbled letters to form words from this unit. Arrange the circled letters to form a surprise answer.

1

ARCSERCK

BEATSELEVG

SHIF

ANSWER: _______________________________________

2

DEARB

LIMK

ESHECE

ANSWER: _______________________________________

WORD MAZES

To find your way out of each maze, follow words from the unit from START to FINISH.
The words can go from left-to-right, from right-to-left, upward, downward or diagonally.

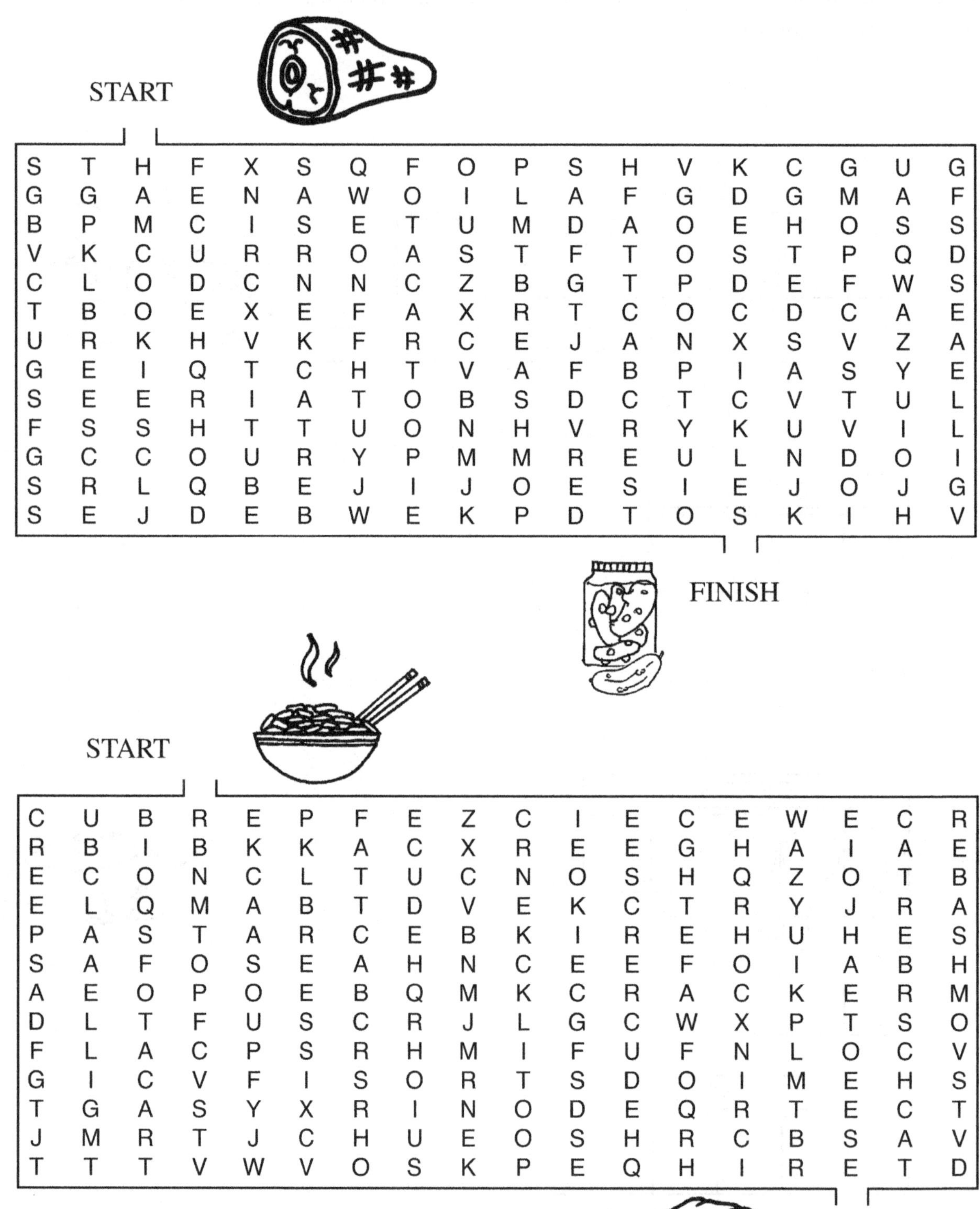

MAGIC WORD

Using words from the unit, complete the fill in the blanks exercise below. When you fill in those words on the chart an extra word will appear in the box.

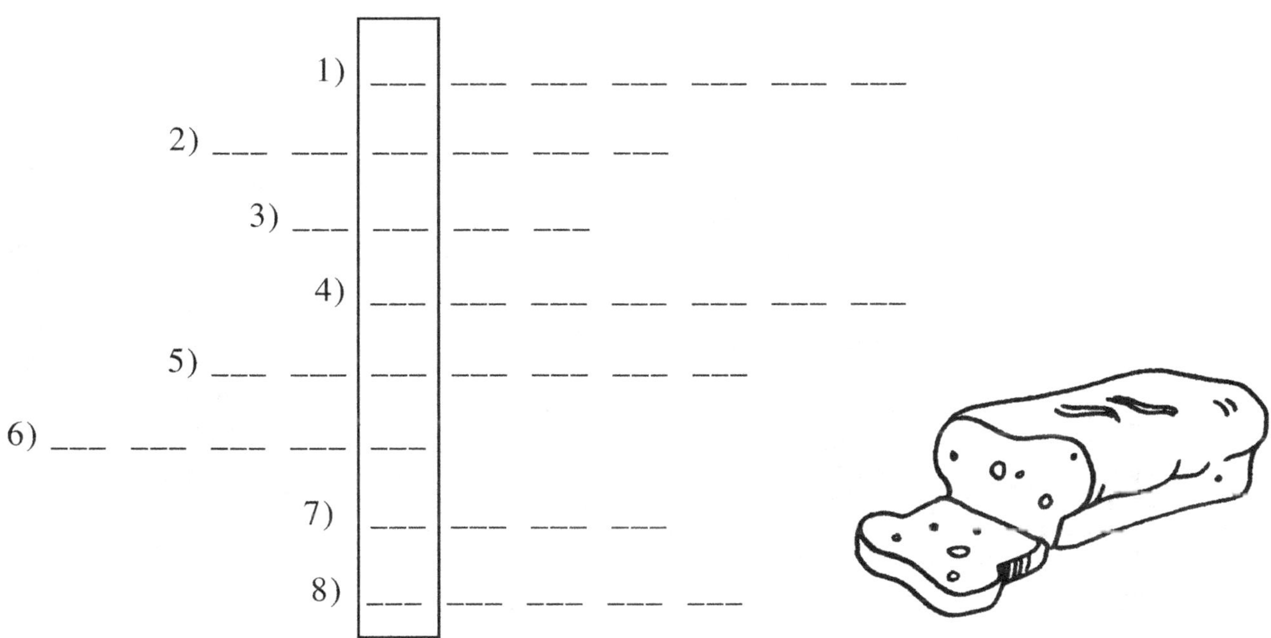

1) Some kinds of _____________________ are sour.

2) _____________________ is a common breakfast food.

3) _____________________ can be fried, baked or broiled.

4) Whenever I eat _____________________, I wear a bib.

5) I love the smell of freshly baked _____________________.

6) _____________________ comes from pigs.

7) My mom likes her _____________________ scrambled.

8) They usually eat a _____________________ on Sunday.

MAGIC WORD: _____________________

EIGHT MISTAKES

There are 8 things missing from Picture Two that can be found in Picture One. Find the missing items and write them down.

1 _______________________________

2 _______________________________

3 _______________________________

4 _______________________________

5 _______________________________

6 _______________________________

7 _______________________________

8 _______________________________

CROSSWORD PUZZLE

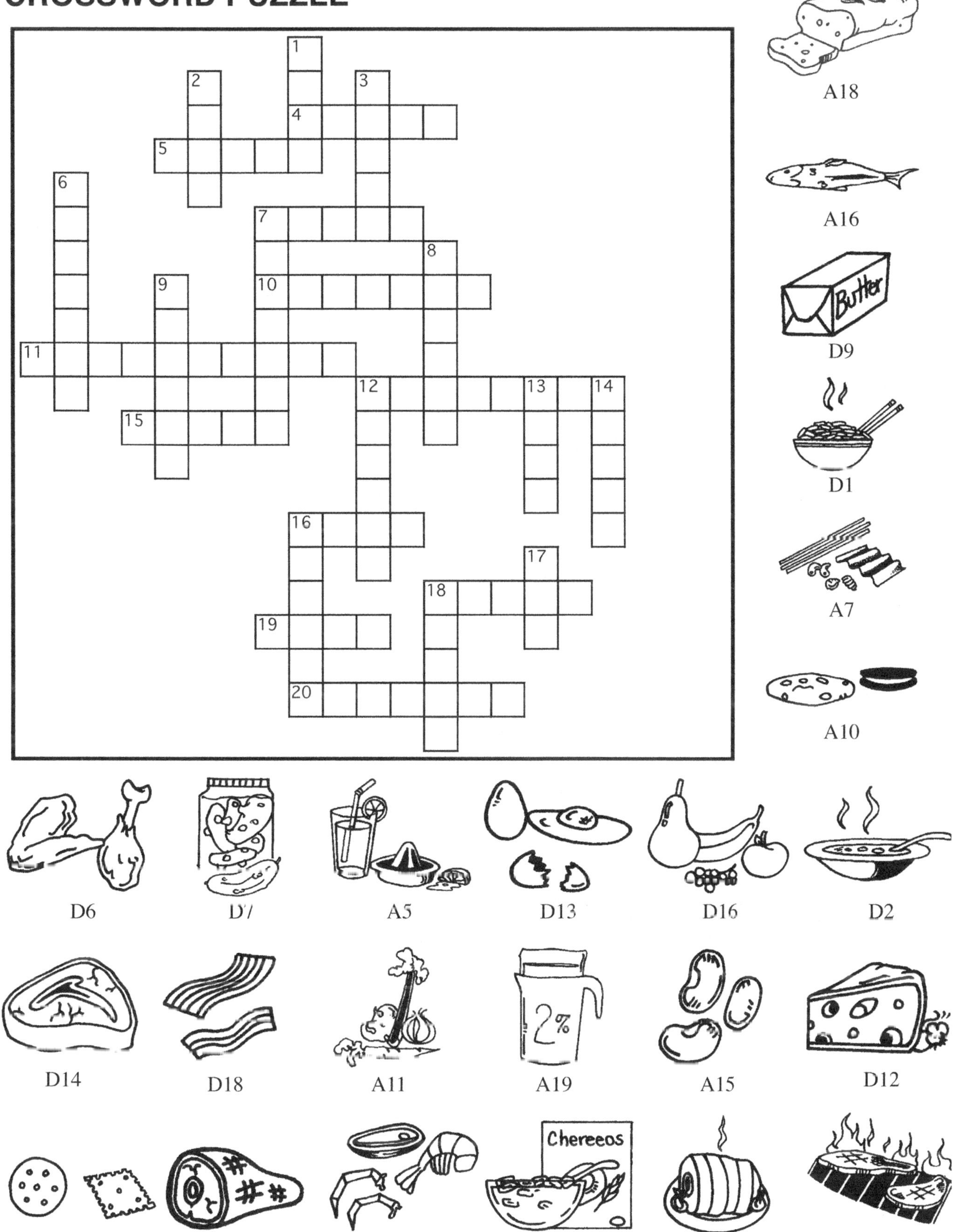

FIND-THE-WORDS PUZZLE

You will find all the words from this unit hidden in the box below. Find each word and circle all its letters. To find the words you may have to read from left-to-right, from right-to-left, upward, downward or diagonally.

V	O	K	P	I	C	K	L	E	S	Y	F	I	S	H	M
C	E	I	V	U	I	D	E	P	P	R	S	O	O	H	E
O	G	G	B	U	Y	F	R	I	U	D	A	U	U	E	N
O	G	G	E	S	T	W	W	I	C	A	C	T	P	S	O
K	S	U	X	T	F	S	T	C	E	M	A	H	I	W	E
I	F	F	F	E	A	S	Z	A	Y	V	O	H	G	S	F
E	G	P	T	A	B	B	Q	T	U	I	C	C	E	A	T
S	U	A	B	K	U	V	L	N	D	D	K	E	T	L	E
A	N	S	D	M	D	Y	T	E	A	E	H	U	I	L	S
R	E	T	T	U	B	M	A	K	S	C	I	C	M	O	R
O	D	A	W	U	O	F	C	C	E	E	N	K	E	W	E
A	G	S	B	Y	N	Y	J	I	A	R	H	M	I	L	K
S	Y	S	E	T	O	F	U	H	F	E	I	E	A	S	C
T	V	C	A	F	C	L	I	C	O	A	S	R	N	S	A
U	I	E	N	D	A	D	C	B	O	L	M	B	D	E	R
R	H	A	S	X	B	R	E	A	D	I	S	P	O	H	C

BACON	FRUITS
BEANS	HAM
BREAD	JUICE
BUTTER	MILK
CEREAL	PASTA
CHEESE	PICKLES
CHICKEN	RICE
CHOPS	ROAST
COOKIES	SEAFOOD
CRACKERS	SOUP
EGGS	STEAK
FISH	VEGETABLES

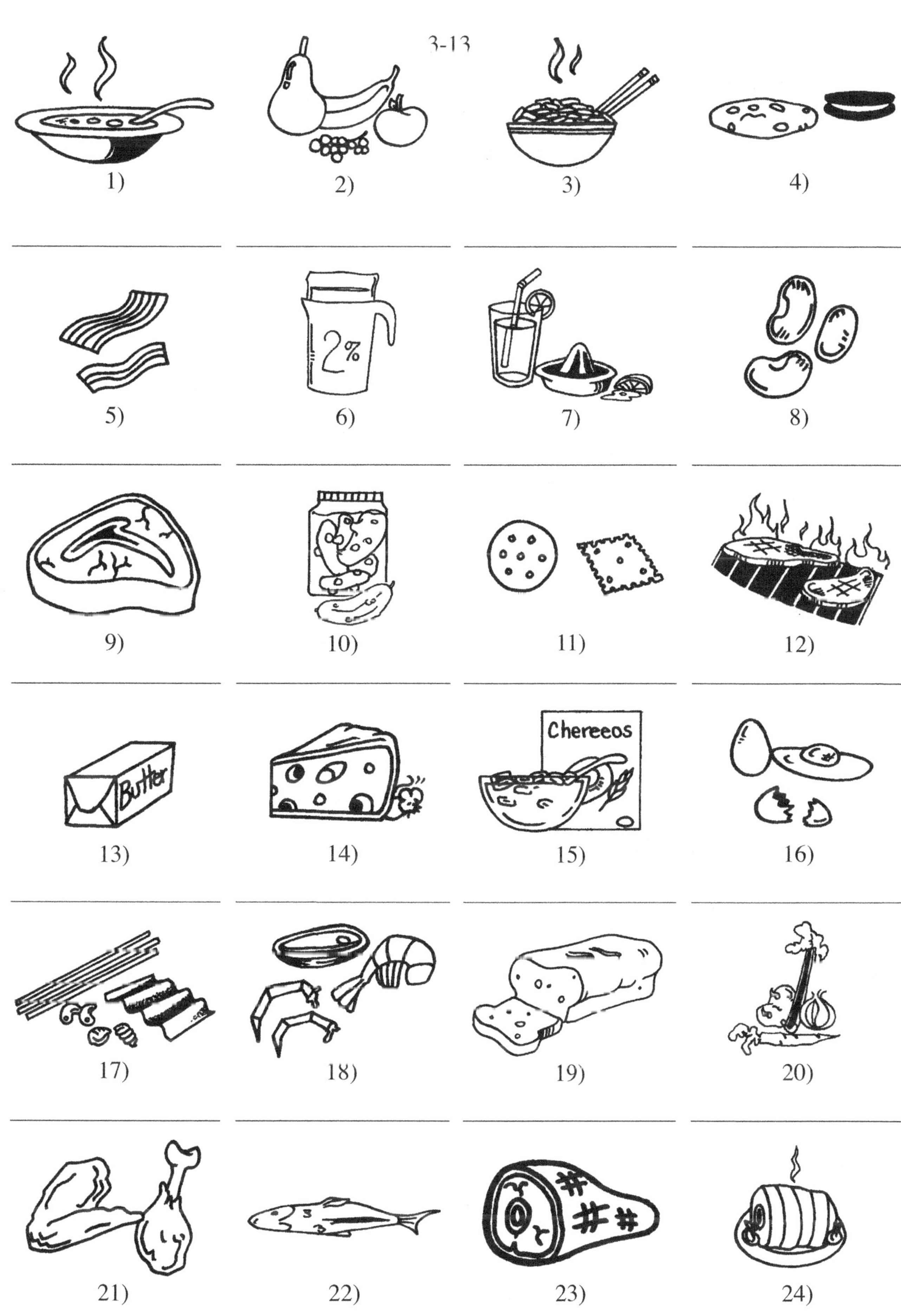

1) 2) 3) 4)

5) 6) 7) 8)

9) 10) 11) 12)

13) 14) 15) 16)

17) 18) 19) 20)

21) 22) 23) 24)

ANSWER KEY

DRAWINGS Page 4

1) soup 2) milk 3) bread 4) pasta 5) chicken 6) juice 7) cheese 8) ham 9) butter 10) crackers 11) cereal 12) chops 13) bacon 14) fish 15) fruits 16) beans 17) vegetables 18) cookies 19) seafood 20) roast 21) rice 22) pickles 23) eggs 24) steak

ORDERING

1) bacon 2) beans 3) bread 4) butter 5) cereal 6) cheese 7) chicken 8) chops 9) cookies 10) crackers 11) eggs 12) fish 13) fruits 14) ham 15) juice 16) milk 17) pasta 18) pickles 19) rice 20) roast 21) seafood 22) soup 23) steak 24) vegetables

QUIZ

1) fish, seafood
2) beans, steak, bread, juice, cheese, soup, roast, seafood, fruits, cookies, cereal
3)

DASHES

1) chicken 2) soup 3) beans 4) roast 5) fruits 6) cereal 7) fish 8) bacon 9) juice 10) steak 11) cheese 12) bread 13) ham 14) seafood 15) cookies 16) chops 17) butter 18) vegetables 19) rice 20) pickles 21) crackers 22) milk 23) eggs 24) pasta

WORD SPIRAL

1) soup 2) fruits 3) rice 4) cookies 5) bacon 6) milk 7) juice 8) beans 9) steak 10) pickles 11) crackers 12) chops 13) butter 14) cheese 15) cereal 16) eggs 17) pasta 18) seafood 19) bread 20) vegetables 21) chicken 22) fish 23) ham 24) roast

WORD MAZES

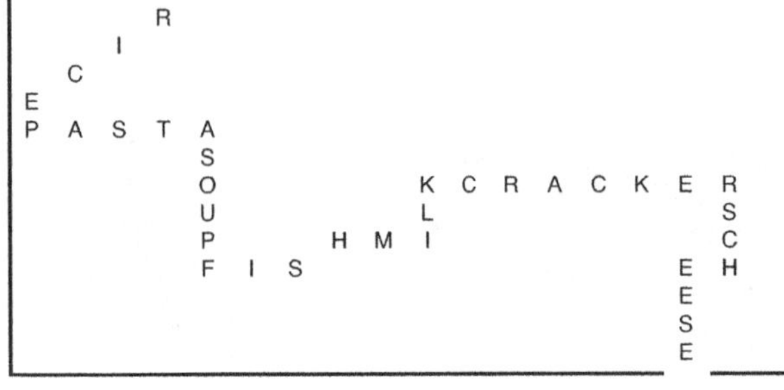

SCRAMBLES

1) breakfast 2) scrambled

EIGHT MISTAKES

1) "4" missing from sign 2) 25¢ missing from price tag 3) broken egg missing 4) man's ear 5) word "butter" missing 6) seam on rice bag 7) lines on fish tail 8) "eye" on potato next to stick of celery

FIND-THE-WORDS PUZZLE

```
V         P   I   C   K   L   E   S           F       I   S   H
C   E                                       R               O
O   G   G                           U                       U
O   G       E   S               I                           P
K   S           T               T           M   A   H
I               E   A   S                                       S
E       P       A       B                                   E
S       A       K           L   N                       E
        S                       E               H
R   E   T   T   U   B           K   S   C
O       A                       C   E   E
A       B       N       J   I   A   R           M   I   L
S       E       O       U   H   F   E
T   C   A       C       I   C   O   A                   A
    I   N       A           C   O   L                   R
R           S       B   R   E   A   D           S   P   O   H   C
```

Unit 4: Adjectives

SENTENCES

1. The little mouse was looking for something to eat.
2. I've decided to lift weights because I am so weak.
3. My cat's fur is soft.
4. The pig is fat.
5. After lifting weights I became strong enough to lift 1,000 pounds.
6. A swan is beautiful.
7. With my magnifying glass I can get a closer look at a tiny ant.
8. The loudspeaker made his voice loud.
9. The toad has ugly warts.
10. The knife is sharp enough to cut a human hair in two.
11. The water was too cold for swimming.
12. Compared to a giraffe, a mouse is short.
13. Rabbits can move fast.
14. Compared to a mouse, a giraffe is tall.
15. Garbage is often smelly, which means it stinks.
16. A coconut has a hard shell.
17. A crane is a bird with thin legs.
18. Mean dogs bark and growl.
19. Elephants are big animals.
20. My new nylons make my legs feel smooth.
21. Our new puppy is friendly.
22. Turtles are slow moving animals.
23. An emery board has a rough sandpaper surface.
24. It is hot in the desert.

1) little

2) weak

3) soft

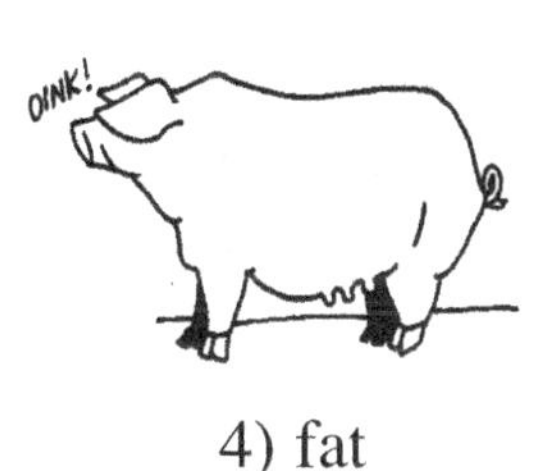

4) fat

5) strong

6) beautiful

7) tiny

8) loud

9) ugly

10) sharp

11) cold

12) short

13) fast

14) tall

15) smelly

16) hard

17) thin

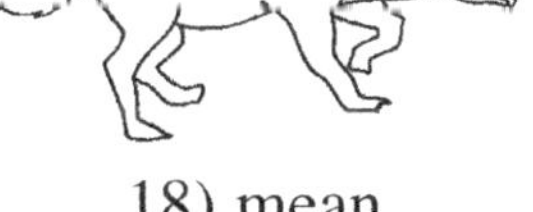

18) mean

19) big

20) smooth

21) friendly

22) slow

23) rough

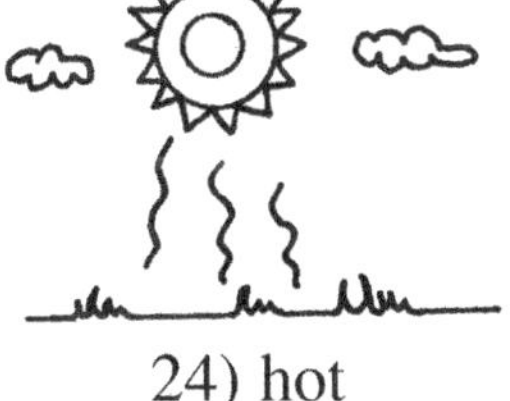

24) hot

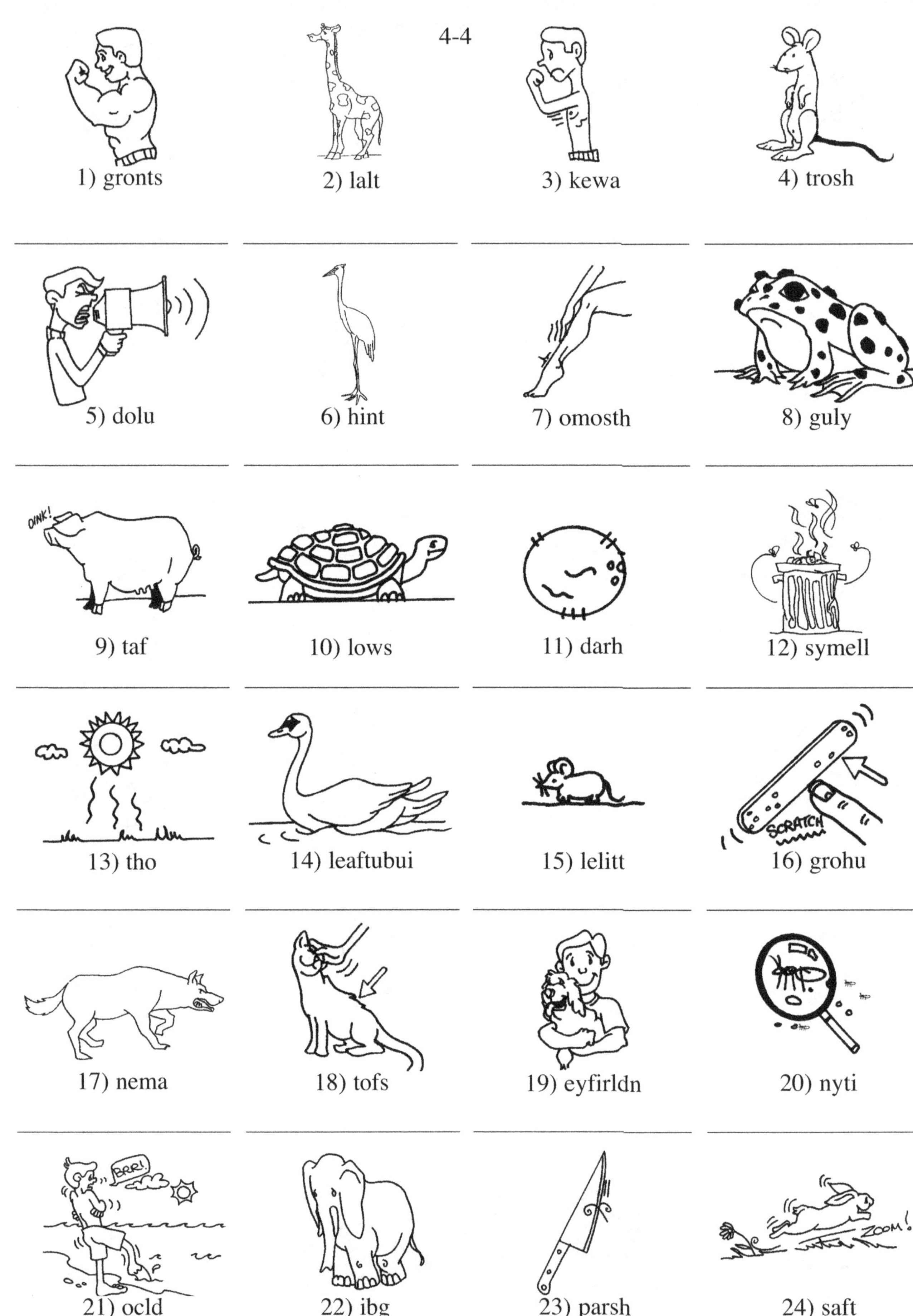

1) gronts
2) lalt
3) kewa
4) trosh
5) dolu
6) hint
7) omosth
8) guly
9) taf
10) lows
11) darh
12) symell
13) tho
14) leaftubui
15) lelitt
16) grohu
17) nema
18) tofs
19) eyfirldn
20) nyti
21) ocld
22) ibg
23) parsh
24) saft

ORDERING

Put the words in alphabetical order.

thin	sharp	hard	fast
fat	loud	soft	slow
tall	smelly	big	beautiful
short	cold	hot	ugly
strong	little	rough	friendly
weak	tiny	smooth	mean

1) _______________________ 13) _______________________

2) _______________________ 14) _______________________

3) _______________________ 15) _______________________

4) _______________________ 16) _______________________

5) _______________________ 17) _______________________

6) _______________________ 18) _______________________

7) _______________________ 19) _______________________

8) _______________________ 20) _______________________

9) _______________________ 21) _______________________

10) ______________________ 22) _______________________

11) ______________________ 23) _______________________

12) ______________________ 24) _______________________

QUIZ

1) Using words from the list, describe your best friend.

____

2) a) The word *little* is similar in meaning to what other word from the list? b) It is opposite to what word?

____

3) The letters 'gh' in the word rough make the same sound as what letter? Can you think of other words that use 'gh' in the same way?

____

DASHES

Complete each word by adding the missing letters. Each dash represents a letter.

1) t _ _ n
2) s _ e _ l _
3) s _ _ o _ g
4) f _ t
5) m _ a _
6) f _ _ t
7) h _ _
8) f r _ _ n _ _ y
9) s _ _ w
1 0) s _ a _ p
1 1) s h _ _ t
1 2) t _ n _

1 3) h _ _ d
1 4) r _ u _ h
1 5) b _ _ _ t _ _ _ l
1 6) s _ _ t
1 7) s _ _ o _ _
1 8) u _ _ y
1 9) b _ _
2 0) c _ l _
2 1) w e _ _
2 2) t _ _ l
2 3) l _ _ t _ _
2 4) l _ u _

WORD SPIRAL

Following the spiral towards the center, circle all the vocabulary words from this unit.

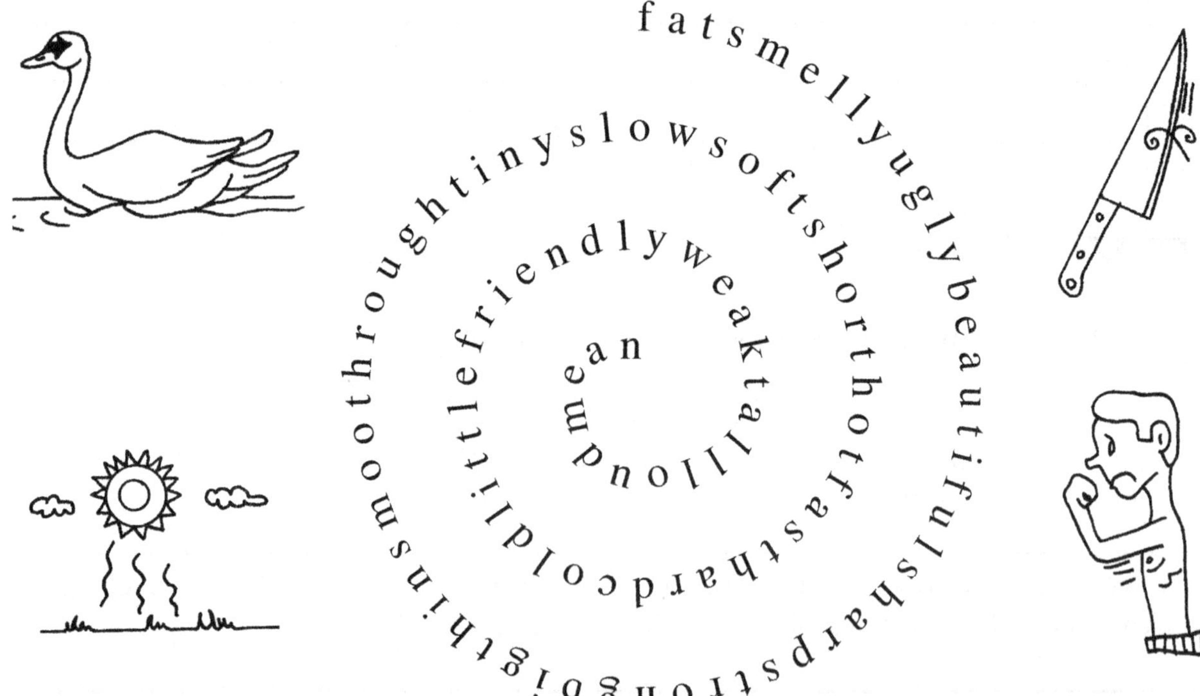

SCRAMBLES

Unscramble the jumbled letters to form words from this unit. Arrange the circled letters to form a surprise answer.

1

PHRAS

NEMA

FABITLUUE

ANSWER: _______________________________________

2

AKEW

LYNREFID

GORUII

ANSWER: _______________________________________

WORD MAZES

To find your way out of each maze, follow words from the unit from START to FINISH. The words can go from left-to-right, from right-to-left, upward, downward or diagonally.

START

```
K  I  R  L  A  T  Y  K  K  A  T  U  O  G  O  I  F  A
L  U  A  O  R  O  H  D  D  A  S  R  I  D  I  P  S  C
S  O  N  A  U  S  N  U  U  D  F  W  P  R  P  W  S  T
A  Y  K  O  M  G  U  V  L  F  E  E  W  F  W  E  S  C
S  H  G  U  D  S  H  M  P  G  I  R  E  H  E  C  V  O
A  G  P  E  A  A  H  N  N  H  B  R  C  B  C  A  B  I
M  R  O  S  C  R  I  E  E  J  U  H  K  V  O  A  Y  P
I  M  L  B  K  D  N  R  R  J  E  N  D  L  Y  L  H  W
N  N  I  M  E  B  B  T  T  I  B  K  T  O  L  I  N  E
B  V  G  U  R  I  G  F  R  L  G  A  P  I  A  T  U  C
T  C  F  Q  T  T  A  L  E  W  H  C  U  I  T  T  S  I
R  X  E  W  Y  V  L  A  S  R  Y  T  I  N  E  L  K  R
E  D  Q  E  E  B  S  S  A  I  T  C  F  Y  O  H  K  E
```

FINISH

START

```
H  E  L  S  P  O  E  N  A  S  S  A  A  L  R  S  F  I
E  K  W  Y  A  R  C  I  R  K  K  A  L  P  T  H  G  N
E  D  R  U  Y  U  F  I  T  U  A  E  B  P  R  A  H  B
H  C  I  L  L  T  A  T  F  U  U  D  U  Y  L  E  L  A
I  I  T  U  D  H  U  E  D  V  L  F  L  A  S  I  A  L
N  E  G  J  E  I  S  L  I  M  P  G  U  S  S  N  A  L
B  J  L  O  A  S  E  U  T  N  N  H  J  K  K  A  J  A
A  X  Y  H  R  J  H  Z  B  E  E  J  O  D  D  A  J  S
D  S  S  M  O  O  T  H  W  E  R  J  H  U  D  A  S  K
F  C  H  W  L  J  E  X  B  T  A  I  M  V  L  H  I  D
C  E  U  I  Y  O  D  O  G  F  R  K  S  T  R  O  E  U
R  N  V  L  F  B  I  W  A  L  E  B  I  N  N  N  E  L
I  Z  E  L  F  B  D  H  L  A  S  G  L  E  E  G  H  P
```

FINISH

MAGIC WORD

Using words from the unit, complete the fill in the blanks exercise below. When you fill in those words on the chart an extra word will appear in the box.

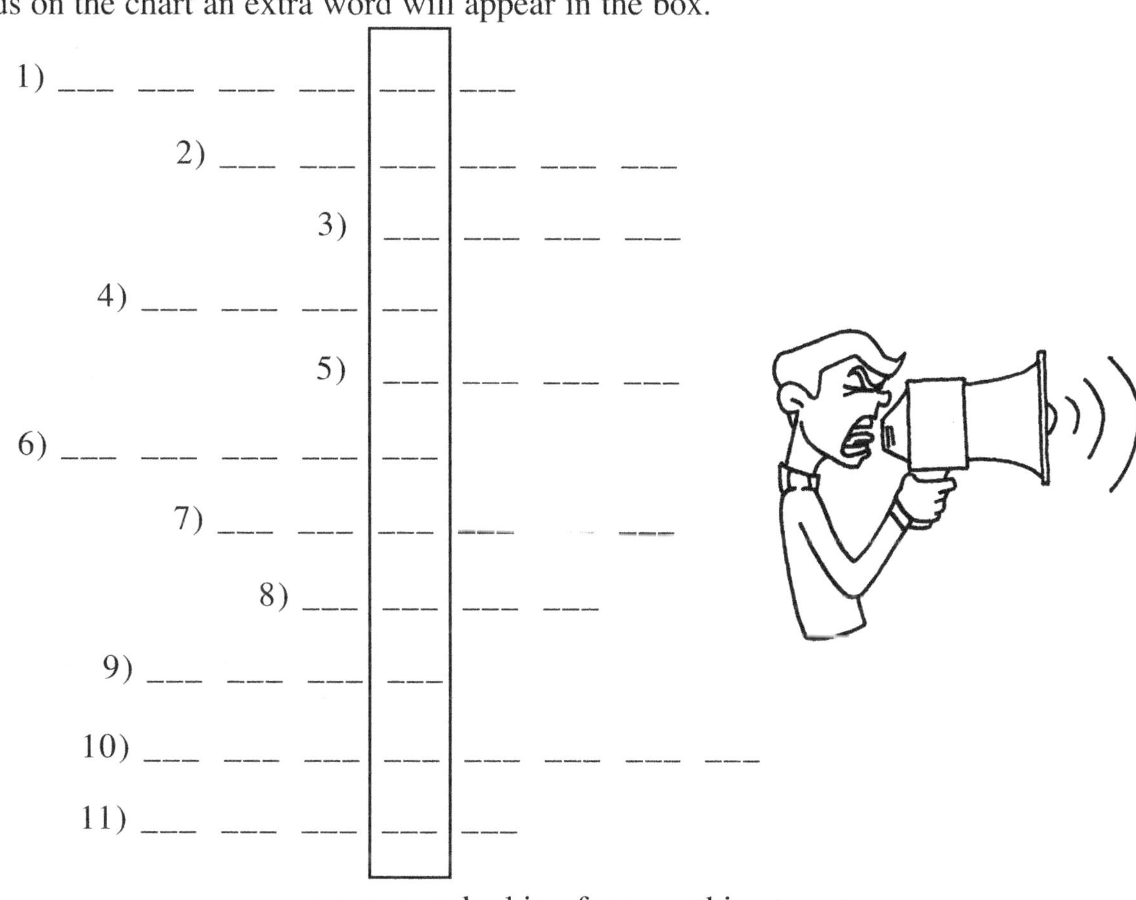

1) The _______________________ mouse was looking for something to eat.

2) My new nylons make my legs feel _______________________.

3) The toad has _______________________ warts.

4) A coconut has a _______________________ shell.

5) My cat's fur is _______________________.

6) The knife is _______________________ enough to cut a human hair in two.

7) Garbage is often _______________________, which means it stinks.

8) Compared to a mouse, a giraffe is _______________________.

9) I've decided to lift weights because I am so _______________________.

10) Our new puppy is _______________________.

11) Compared to a giraffe, a mouse is _______________________.

MAGIC WORD: _______________________

EIGHT MISTAKES

There are 8 things missing from Picture Two that can be found in Picture One. Find the missing items and write them down.

1 ____

2 ____

3 ____

4 ____

5 ____

6 ____

7 ____

8 ____

CROSSWORD PUZZLE

FIND-THE-WORDS PUZZLE

You will find all the words from this unit hidden in the box below. Find each word and circle all its letters. To find the words you may have to read from left-to-right, from right-to-left, upward, downward or diagonally.

```
B  X  V  T  H  D  R  F  E  L  I  T  T  L  E  G
E  I  R  A  I  I  D  R  R  A  T  A  B  A  N  E
A  U  G  L  J  W  W  I  F  N  N  W  C  O  F  E
U  L  K  L  K  M  E  E  D  H  D  S  R  A  S  J
T  B  I  U  L  E  A  N  T  O  T  T  U  C  A  U
I  H  B  T  D  A  K  D  V  T  S  C  U  A  D  Y
F  U  C  B  D  N  S  L  T  N  O  R  O  U  G  H
U  S  L  O  U  D  D  Y  A  D  F  Q  W  L  D  L
L  O  Z  C  O  T  S  A  F  T  T  N  E  T  O  A
B  T  C  O  L  D  F  C  P  D  L  I  R  I  C  B
H  N  P  B  P  L  M  C  Y  L  I  H  S  N  H  H
U  F  O  H  P  M  H  A  R  D  Y  T  F  Y  E  T
I  G  I  R  P  U  D  Z  D  Z  W  C  R  O  R  O
N  H  A  A  Q  G  E  A  G  O  T  D  V  O  T  O
F  H  A  B  R  L  M  P  L  X  L  F  V  K  H  M
S  D  E  C  M  Y  P  S  M  E  L  L  Y  L  E  S
```

BEAUTIFUL	SHARP
BIG	SHORT
COLD	SLOW
FAST	SMELLY
FAT	SMOOTH
FRIENDLY	SOFT
HARD	STRONG
HOT	TALL
LITTLE	THIN
LOUD	TINY
MEAN	UGLY
ROUGH	WEAK

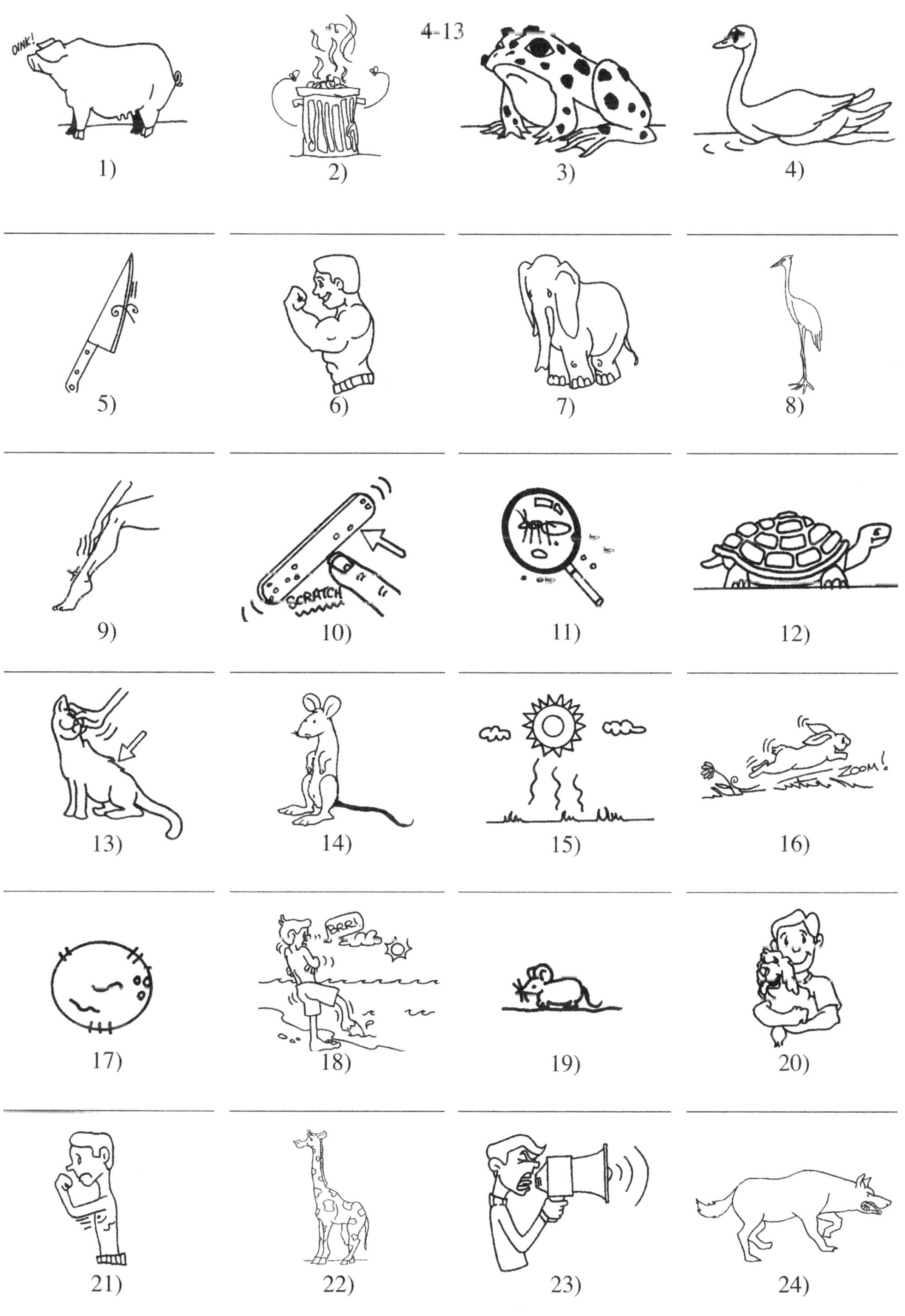

1)

2)

3)

4)

5)

6)

7)

8)

9)

10)

11)

12)

13)

14)

15)

16)

17)

18)

19)

20)

21)

22)

23)

24)

ANSWER KEY

DRAWINGS Page 4

1) strong 2) tall 3) weak 4) short 5) loud 6) thin 7) smooth 8) ugly 9) fat 10) slow 11) hard 12) smelly 13) hot 14) beautiful 15) little 16) rough 17) mean 18) soft 19) friendly 20) tiny 21) cold 22) big 23) sharp 24) fast

ORDERING

1) beautiful 2) big 3) cold 4) fast 5) fat 6) friendly 7) hard 8) hot 9) little 10) loud 11) mean 12) rough 13) sharp 14) short 15) slow 16) smelly 17) smooth 18) soft 19) strong 20) tall 21) thin 22) tiny 23) ugly 24) weak

QUIZ

1) ?
2) a) tiny b) big
3) 'gh' sounds like 'f'; examples incude tough, enough, cough

DASHES

1) thin 2) smelly 3) strong 4) fat 5) mean 6) fast 7) hot 8) friendly 9) slow 10) sharp 11) short 12) tiny 13) hard 14) rough 15) beautiful 16) soft 17) smooth 18) ugly 19) big 20) cold 21) weak 22) tall 23) little 24) loud

WORD SPIRAL

1) fat 2) smelly 3) ugly 4) beautiful 5) sharp 6) strong 7) big 8) thin 9) smooth 10) rough 11) tiny 12) slow 13) soft 14) short 15) hot 16) fast 17) hard 18) cold 19) little 20) friendly 21) weak 22) tall 23) loud 24) mean

WORD MAZES

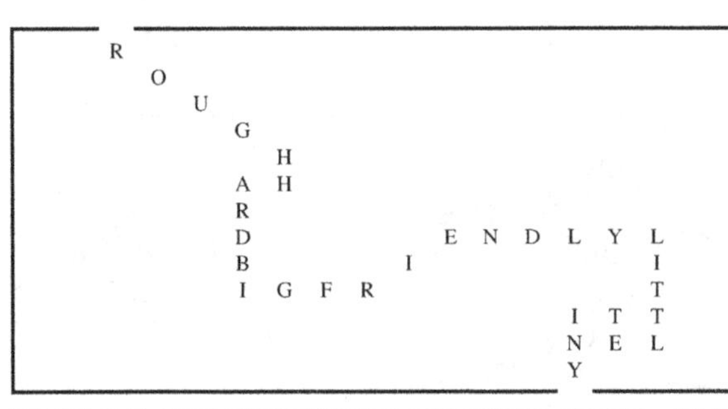

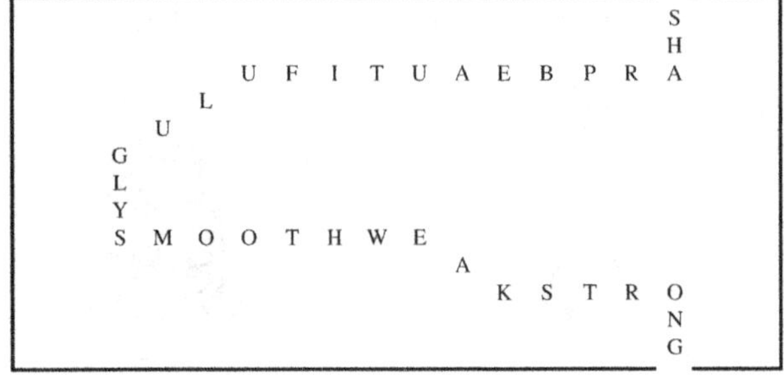

SCRAMBLES

1) elephants 2) growl

EIGHT MISTAKES

1) snake's head 2) elephant's knee 3) airplane propeller
4) dark spot on coconut 5) "BUZZ!" 6) giraffe's horn
7) water drop from plant in front 8) giraffe's tail

FIND-THE-WORDS PUZZLE

```
B        T              F        L  I  T  T  L  E  G
E  I     A              R                          N
A     G  L        W  I              O
U        L     M  E  E     H           R
T        E  A  N     O  T
I        A  K  D  T  S
F        N     L  T     O  R  O  U  G  H
U     L  O  U  D     Y  A  F
L        T  S  A  F     T  N           T
   C  O  L  D              I           I
                          H        N           H
         P     H  A  R  D  T        Y           T
      R  U              W     R                 O
   A     G           O              O           O
 H       L           L                    H  M
S        Y     S  M  E  L  L  Y                 S
```

MAGIC WORD

1) little 2) smooth 3) ugly 4) hard 5) soft 6) sharp 7) smelly 8) tall 9) weak 10) friendly 11) short MAGIC WORD: loudspeaker

CROSSWORD PUZZLE

ACROSS: 2) loud 3) hard 7) smooth 8) fast 9) short 10) big 12) weak 13) ugly 14) tiny 15) friendly 17) smelly 19) thin 20) fat
DOWN: 1) cold 3) hot 4) rough 5) soft 6) strong 7) sharp 9) slow 10) beautiful 11) tall 16) little 18) mean

TEST Page 13

1) fat 2) smelly 3) ugly 4) beautiful 5) sharp 6) strong 7) big 8) thin 9) smooth 10) rough 11) tiny 12) slow 13) soft 14) short 15) hot 16) fast 17) hard 18) cold 19) little 20) friendly 21) weak 22) tall 23) loud 24) mean

Unit 5: Health Care

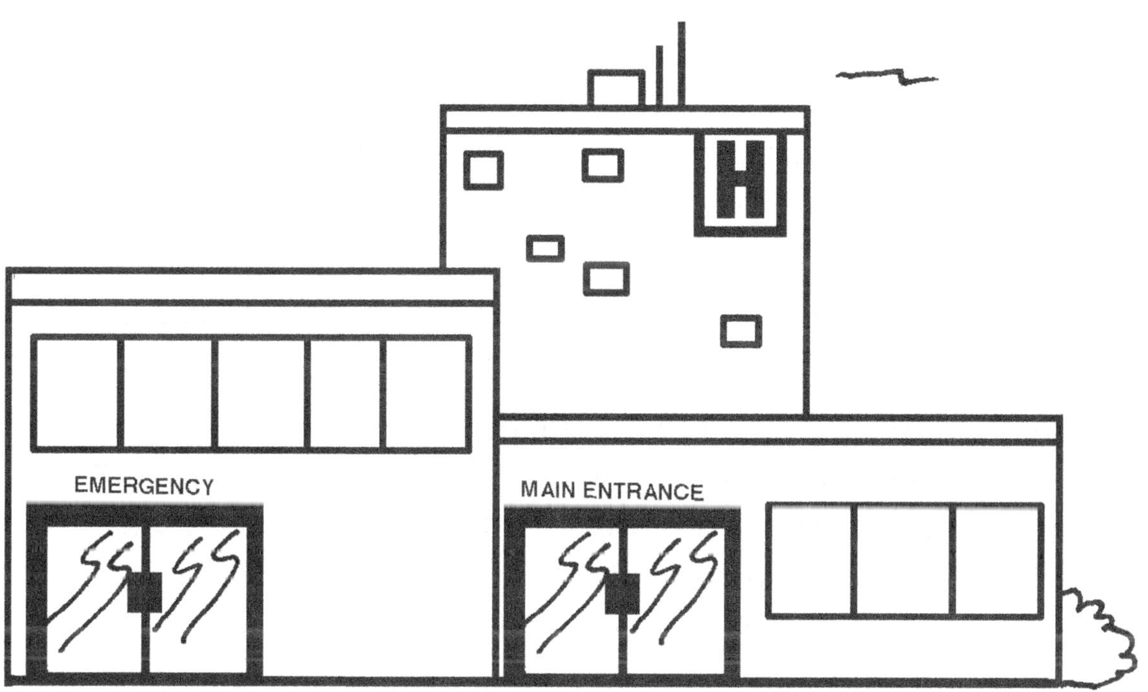

SENTENCES

1. The young boy started to cry when he saw the needle.
2. A nurse assists a doctor.
3. I had my tonsils removed at the hospital.
4. I used my crutches to help me walk after I broke my leg.
5. She slept in a hospital bed after her operation.
6. The nurse put a bandage on my cut leg.
7. Her arm was put in a sling.
8. He is taking pills to relieve his headache.
9. A surgeon removed my grandfather's appendix.
10. The doctor put on rubber gloves before he examined me.
11. My grandmother had an x ray taken after she fell down the stairs.
12. When he had his heart attack he was rushed to emergency.
13. All of my friends signed my cast.
14. A surgical mask is used to stop germs from spreading.
15. I had an operation to repair my knee.
16. A thermometer measures temperature.
17. I needed medicine so the doctor gave me a prescription.
18. My grandmother can't walk so she uses a wheelchair.
19. That deep cut will need stitches.
20. Too much salt is bad for your blood pressure.
21. I was too ill to chew, so I had my food by intravenous.
22. The doctor used a stethoscope to listen to my heart.
23. I go to the doctor once a year for a checkup.
24. The doctor hit my knee with a hammer to test my reflexes.

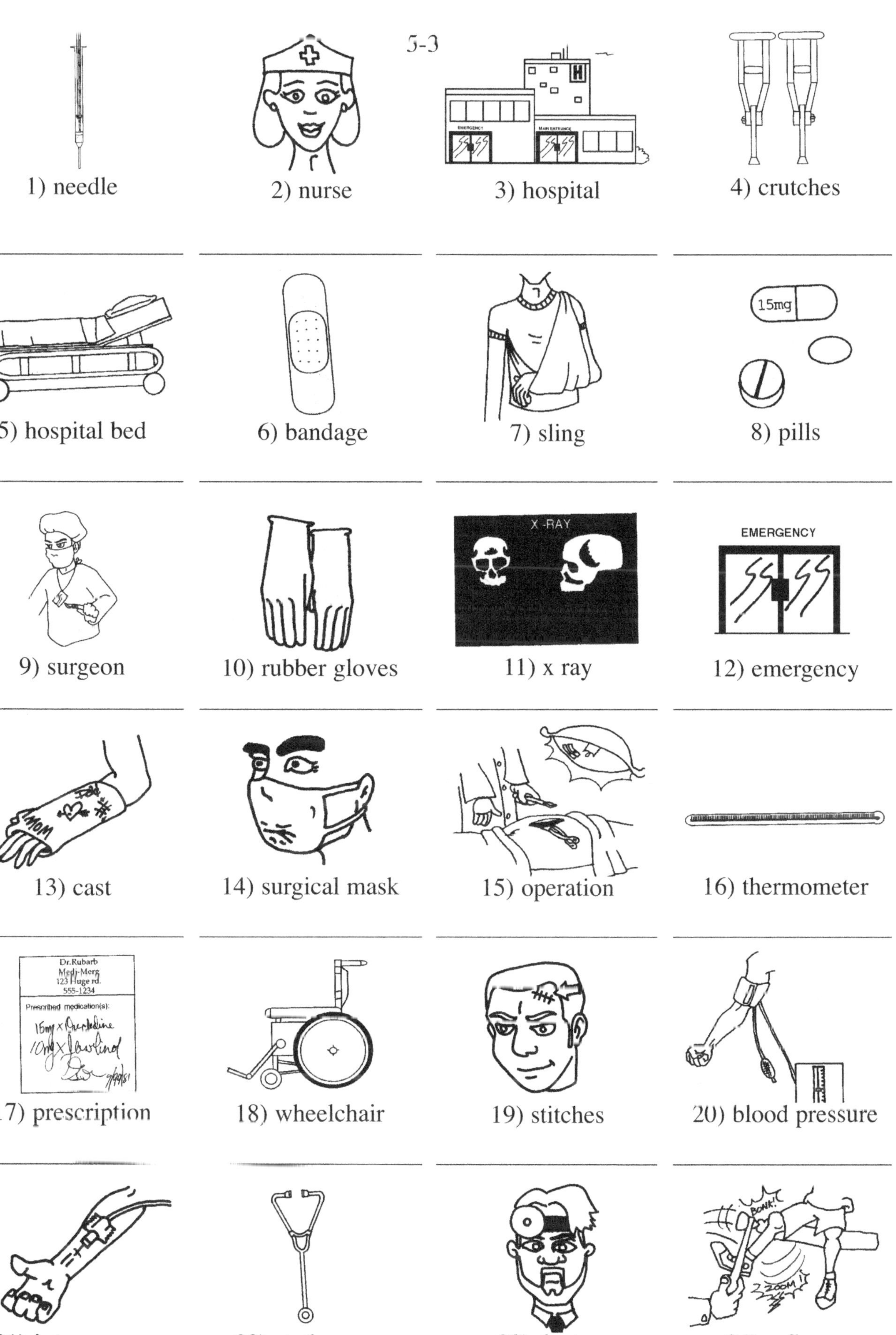
1) needle
2) nurse
3) hospital
4) crutches
5) hospital bed
6) bandage
7) sling
8) pills
9) surgeon
10) rubber gloves
11) x ray
12) emergency
13) cast
14) surgical mask
15) operation
16) thermometer
17) prescription
18) wheelchair
19) stitches
20) blood pressure
21) intravenous
22) stethoscope
23) doctor
24) reflexes

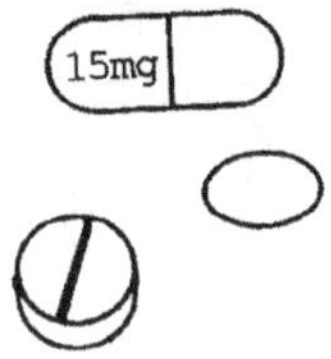

1) lipsl

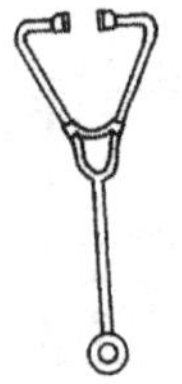

2) tosheepcots

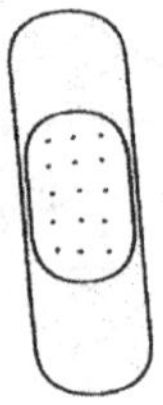

3) neadbag

4) gusnero

5) runes

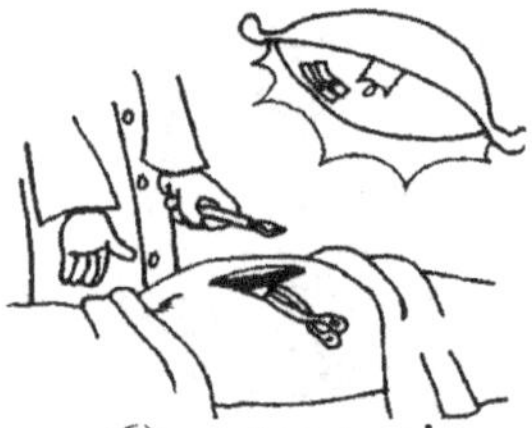

6) notropeai

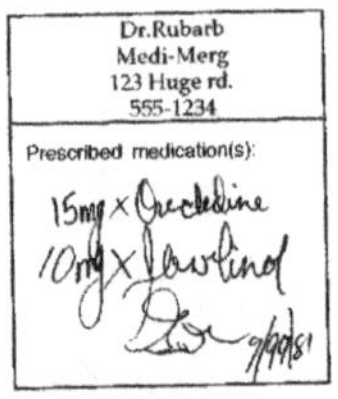

7) stripepronic

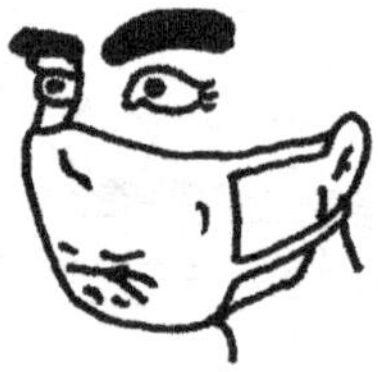

8) lagscrui smak

9) shicsett

10) tacs

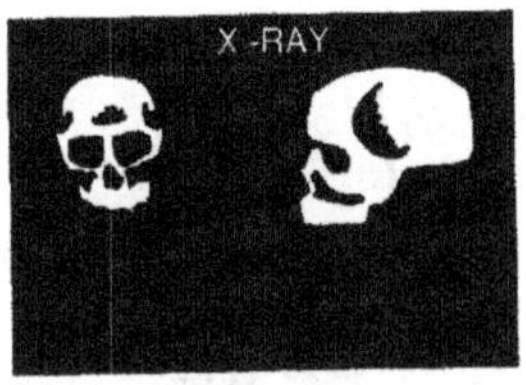

11) ayxr

12) sevonutrain

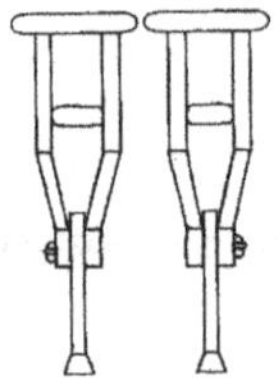

13) chesturc

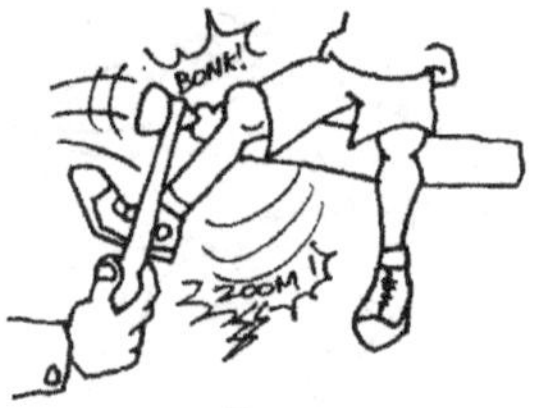

14) fleerxes

15) deelne

16) tdoorc

17) ginsl

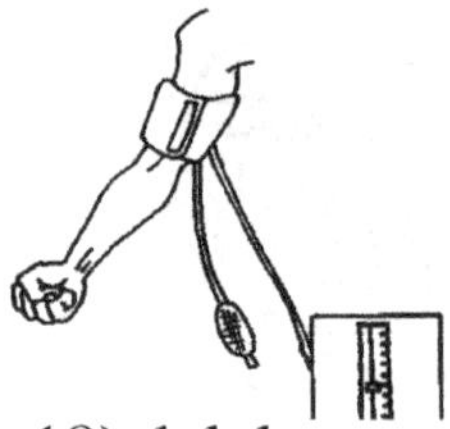

18) dolob sereprus

19) romthemerte

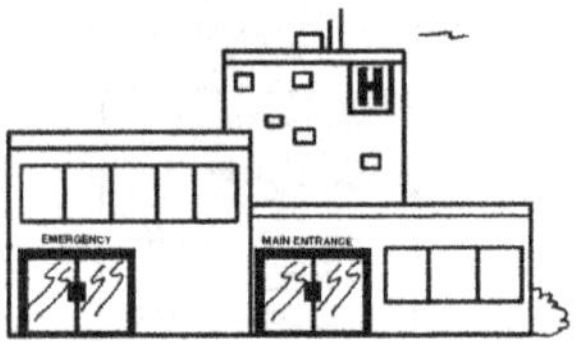

20) shoaltip

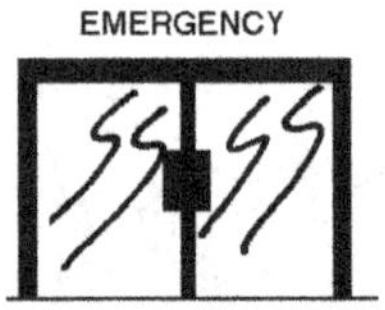

21) geermenyc

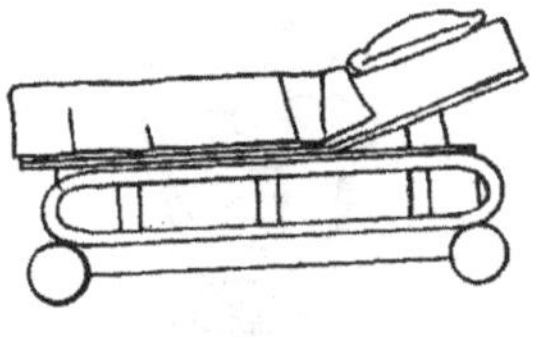

22) poshlait deb

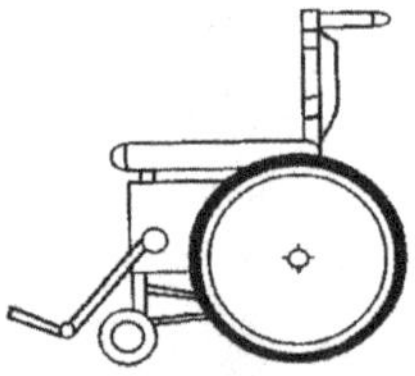

23) rawcelehih

24) bruber slegvo

ORDERING

Put the words in alphabetical order.

stethoscope	blood pressure	bandage	nurse
thermometer	intravenous	cast	hospital
pills	surgeon	crutches	emergency
prescription	stitches	sling	hospital bed
needle	surgical mask	rubber gloves	operation
x ray	wheelchair	doctor	reflexes

1) ________________________ 13) ________________________

2) ________________________ 14) ________________________

3) ________________________ 15) ________________________

4) ________________________ 16) ________________________

5) ________________________ 17) ________________________

6) ________________________ 18) ________________________

7) ________________________ 19) ________________________

8) ________________________ 20) ________________________

9) ________________________ 21) ________________________

10) ________________________ 22) ________________________

11) ________________________ 23) ________________________

12) ________________________ 24) ________________________

QUIZ

1) Using the list above, write down all the health care items that you have had contact with in some way.

____

2) List the words that have only one syllable.

____

3) List the words that have 4 or more syllables.

____

DASHES

Complete each word by adding the missing letters. Each dash represents a letter.

1) n e _ _ l _

2) s u _ _ e _ _

3) s _ e _ h _ s _ o _ e

4) s t _ _ _ h _ s

5) x _ _ y

6) s _ r _ i _ al m _ _ k

7) t _ e _ m _ _ _ t _ r

8) w _ _ e _ _ h _ _ r

9) b _ _ _ d p _ _ _ s _ _ e

10) p _ l _ _

11) i _ _ r _ _ e _ _ us

12) p _ _ _ c _ _ p _ i _ n

13) b _ _ d _ _ e

14) h _ s _ i _ _ l

15) r _ _ b _ _ g _ _ _ e s

16) c _ s _

17) e _ _ r _ _ n _ _

18) h _ s _ _ t _ l b _ _

19) c _ u _ c _ e _

20) d _ _ t _ _

21) o _ _ _ a _ _ _ n

22) s _ _ n _

23) n _ _ s _

24) r e _ _ e _ e s

WORD SPIRAL

Following the spiral towards the center, circle all the vocabulary words from this unit.

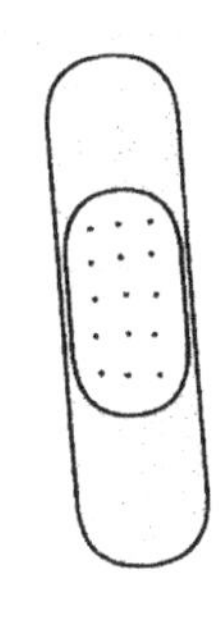

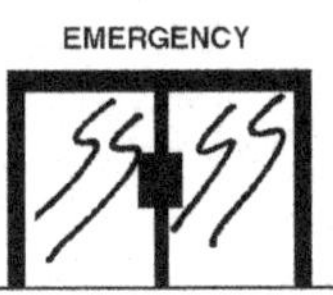

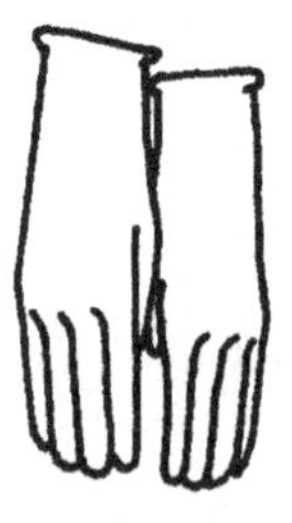

bandagethermometerxrayopera
hospitalnursestethoscopecast
chairpressureneedlereflexessurge
wheelchairhospitalbedcrutche
bloodpressurenoushospitalsling
intravenousscriptionslingdo
venoushospitalslin
prescriptionor
doc

SCRAMBLES

Unscramble the jumbled letters to form words from this unit. Arrange the circled letters to form a surprise answer.

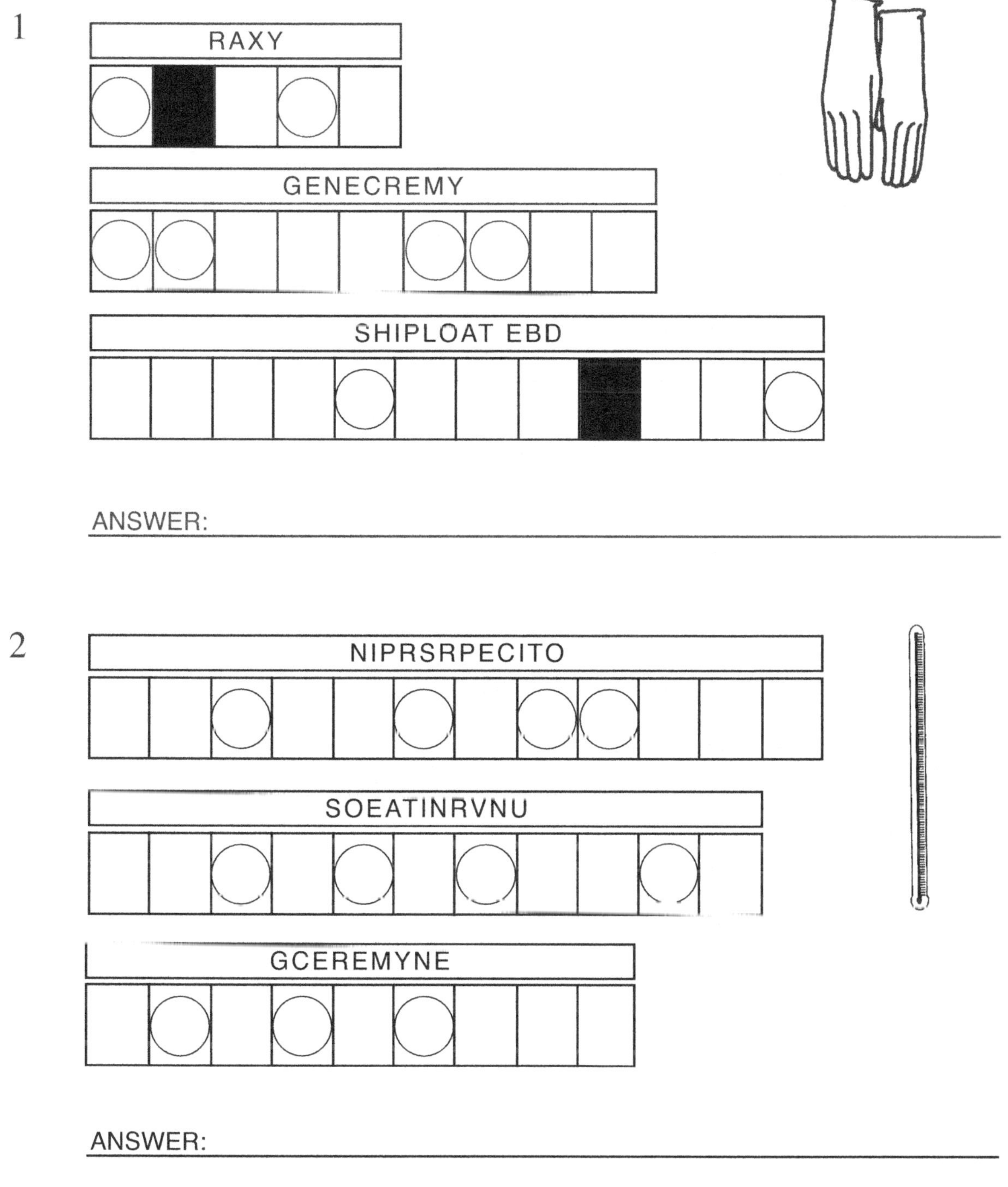

1

RAXY

GENECREMY

SHIPLOAT EBD

ANSWER:

2

NIPRSRPECITO

SOEATINRVNU

GCEREMYNE

ANSWER:

WORD MAZES

To find your way out of each maze, follow words from the unit from START to FINISH.
The words can go from left-to-right, from right-to-left, upward, downward or diagonally.

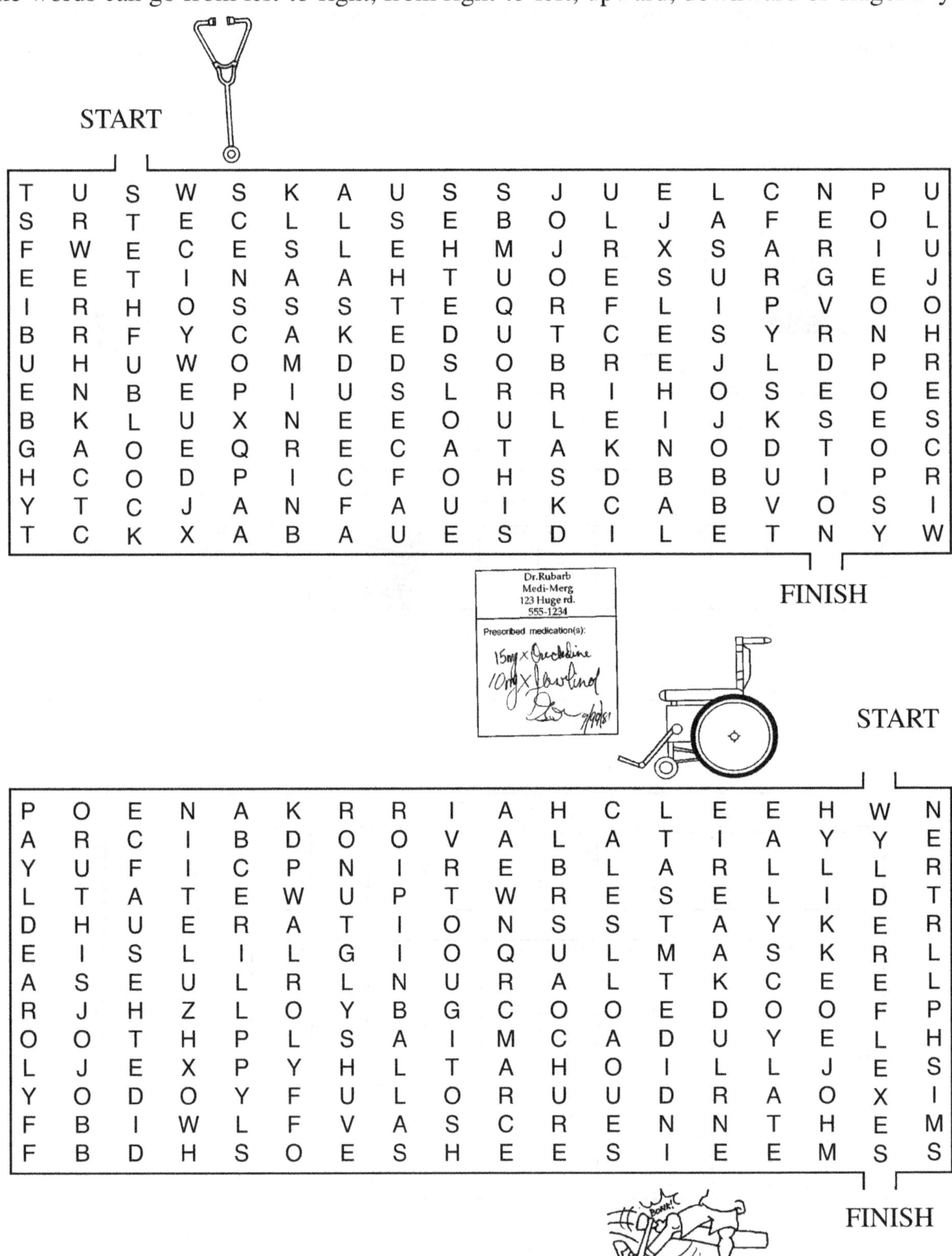

START

```
T U S W S K A U S S J U E L C N P U
S R T E C L L S E B O L J A F E O L
F W E C E S L E H M J R X S A R I U
E E T I N A A H T U O E S U R G E J
I R H O S S S T E Q R F L I P V O O
B R F Y C A K E D U T C E S Y R N H
U H U W O M D D S O B R E J L D P R
E N B E P I U S L R R I H O S E O E
B K L U X N E E O U L E I J K S E S
G A O E Q R E C A T A K N O D T O C
H C O D P I C F O H S D B B U I P R
Y T C J A N F A U I K C A B V O S I
T C K X A B A U E S D I L E T N Y W
```

FINISH

START

```
P O E N A K R R I A H C L E E H W N
A R C I B D O O V A L A T I A Y Y E
Y U F I C P N I R E B L A R L L L R
L T A T E W U G T W R E S E L I D T
D H U E R A T I O N S S T A Y K E R
E I S L I L G L U Q U L M A S K R L
A S E U L R L N G R A L T K C E E L
R J H Z L O Y B I C O O E D O O F P
O O T H P L S A T M C A D U Y E L H
L J E X P Y H L O A H O I L L J E S
Y O D O Y F U L S R U U D R A O X I
F B I W L F V A H C R E N A O H E M
F B D H S O E S H E E S S E E M S S
```

FINISH

MAGIC WORD

Using words from the unit, complete the fill in the blanks exercise below. When you fill in those words on the chart an extra word will appear in the box.

1) ___ ___ ___ ___ ___ ___ | ___ | ___ ___ ___ ___

2) ___ ___ ___ ___ ___ ___ ___ | ___ | ___ ___ ___ ___

3) ___ ___ ___ | ___ | ___ ___ ___ ___ ___

4) ___ ___ | ___ | ___ ___ ___

5) ___ | ___ | ___ ___

6) ___ | ___ ___ ___ ___ ___

7) ___ ___ ___ ___ | ___ | ___ ___ ___

8) ___ ___ ___ ___ ___ ___ ___ | ___ | ___ ___ ___

9) ___ ___ ___ | ___ | ___ ___ ___

1) The doctor used a _____________________ to listen to my heart.

2) I needed medicine so the doctor gave me a _____________________.

3) When he had his heart attack he was rushed to _____________________.

4) The young boy started to cry when he saw the _____________________.

5) All of my friends signed my _____________________.

6) I go to the _____________________ once a year for a checkup.

7) I had my tonsils removed at the _____________________.

8) I was too ill to chew, so I had my food by _____________________.

9) A _____________________ removed my grandfather's appendix.

MAGIC WORD: _____________________

EIGHT MISTAKES

There are 8 things missing from Picture Two that can be found in Picture One. Find the missing items and write them down.

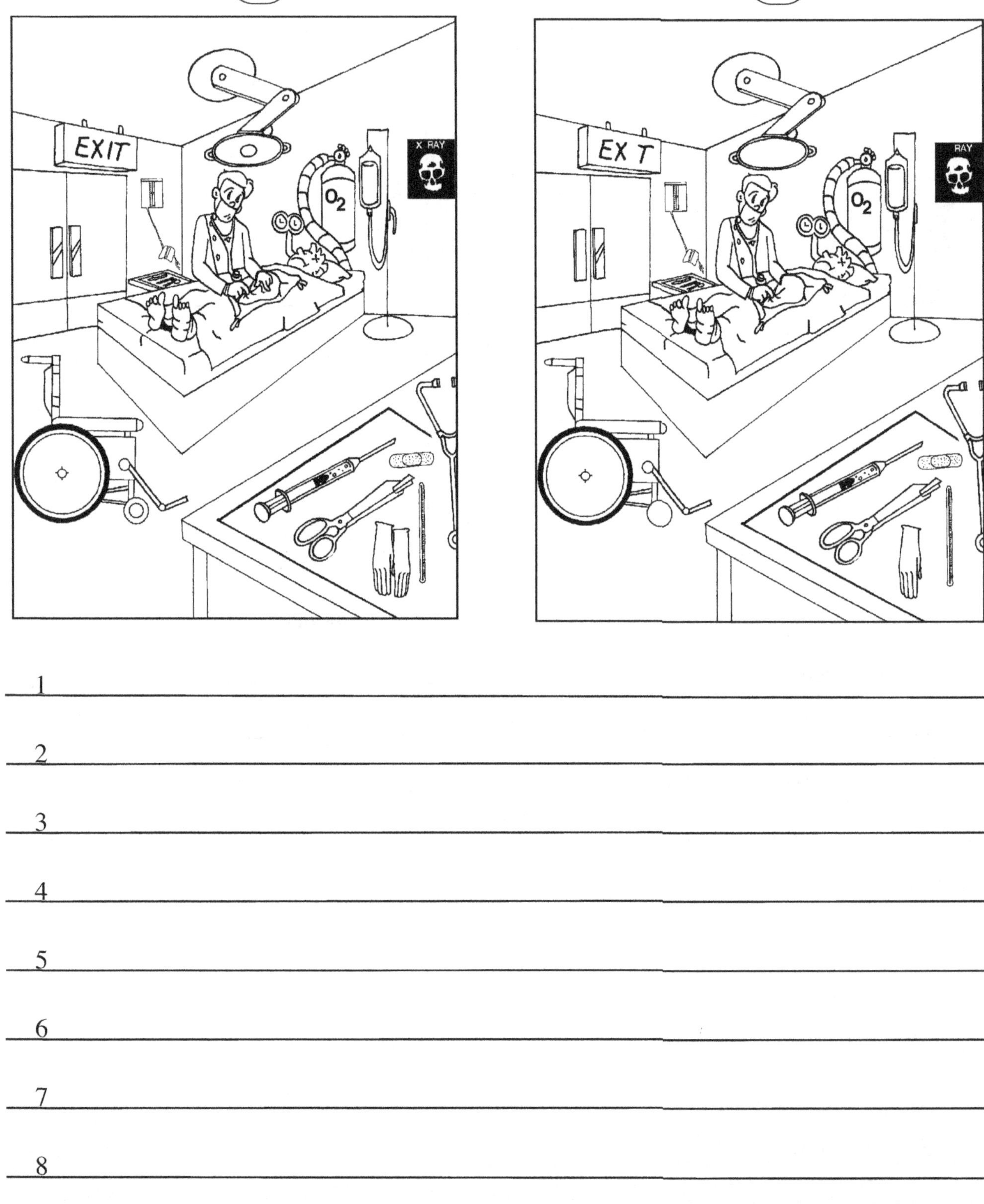

1 _______________________________

2 _______________________________

3 _______________________________

4 _______________________________

5 _______________________________

6 _______________________________

7 _______________________________

8 _______________________________

CROSSWORD PUZZLE

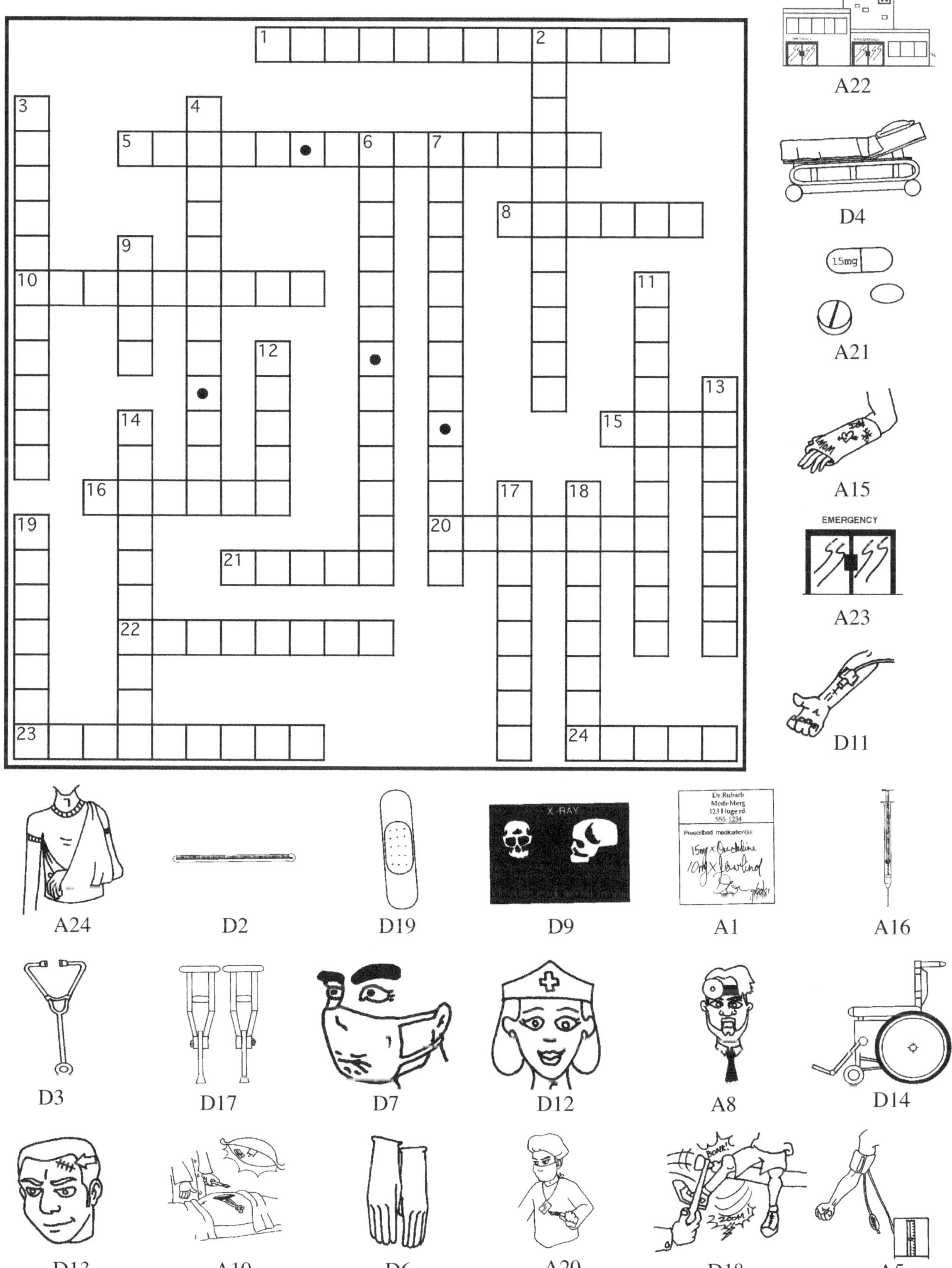

FIND-THE-WORDS PUZZLE

You will find all the words from this unit hidden in the box below. Find each word and circle all its letters. To find the words you may have to read from left-to-right, from right-to-left, upward, downward or diagonally.

```
R  U  B  B  E  R  G  L  O  V  E  S  H  S  I  I
H  R  M  B  A  N  D  A  G  E  N  L  I  L  N  S
O  E  C  R  U  T  C  H  E  S  D  Y  N  I  T  S
S  A  A  L  A  T  I  P  S  O  H  C  T  N  R  E
P  R  E  S  C  R  I  P  T  I  O  N  H  G  A  R
I  S  E  H  C  T  I  T  S  A  E  E  E  H  V  U
T  L  R  O  B  L  S  S  E  P  I  G  R  E  E  S
A  Y  C  C  L  U  M  S  O  D  A  R  M  N  N  S
L  L  E  S  R  S  E  C  L  O  E  E  O  O  O  E
B  I  L  G  E  X  S  A  A  C  L  M  M  I  U  R
E  K  E  H  E  O  A  S  U  T  D  E  E  T  S  P
D  O  B  L  H  E  K  T  G  O  E  S  T  A  N  D
N  E  F  T  C  H  E  M  H  R  E  O  E  R  U  O
I  E  E  U  A  E  Y  A  R  X  N  T  R  E  R  O
R  T  R  W  H  E  E  L  C  H  A  I  R  P  S  L
S  U  R  G  I  C  A  L  M  A  S  K  K  O  E  B
```

BANDAGE	PILLS
BLOOD PRESSURE	PRESCRIPTION
CAST	REFLEXES
CRUTCHES	RUBBER GLOVES
DOCTOR	SLING
EMERGENCY	STETHOSCOPE
HOSPITAL	STITCHES
HOSPITAL BED	SURGEON
INTRAVENOUS	SURGICAL MASK
NEEDLE	THERMOMETER
NURSE	WHEELCHAIR
OPERATION	X RAY

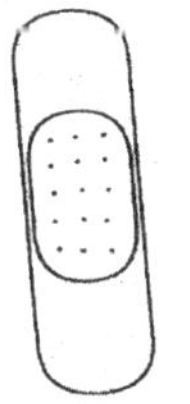

5 13

1)

2)

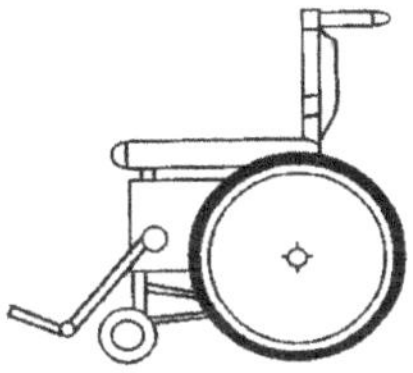

3)

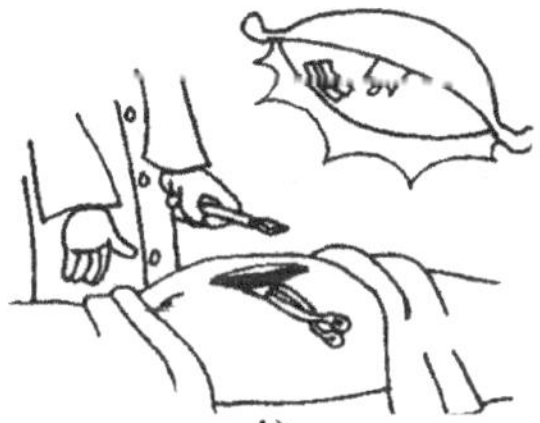

4)

5)

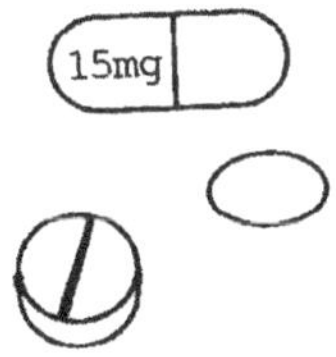

6)

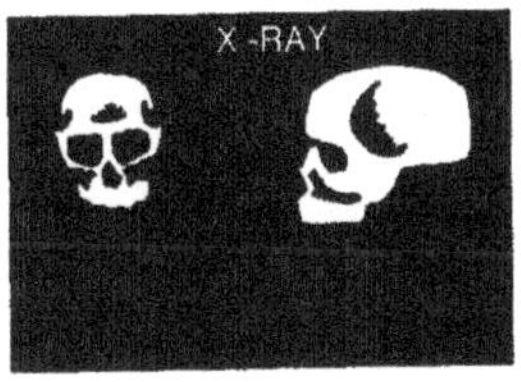

7)

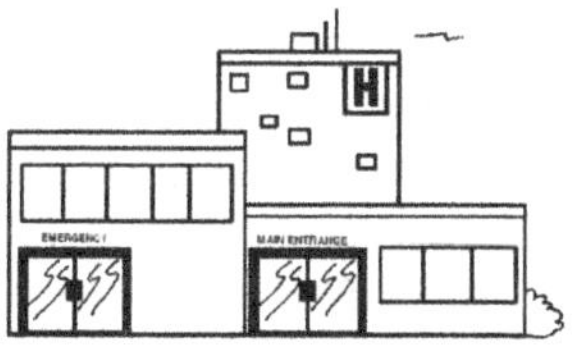

8)

9)

10)

11)

12)

13)

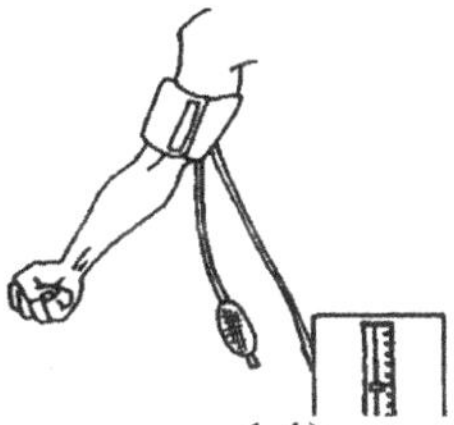

14)

15)

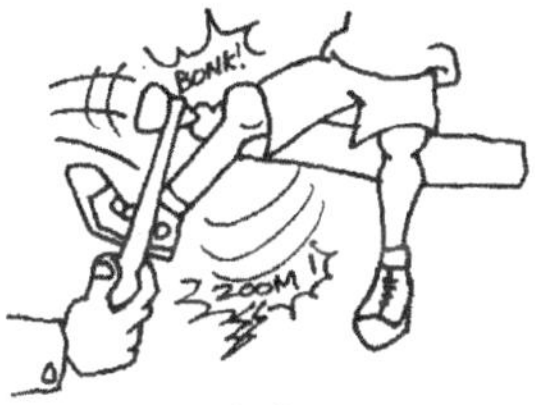

16)

17)

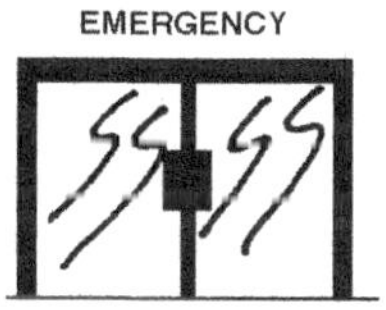

18)

19)

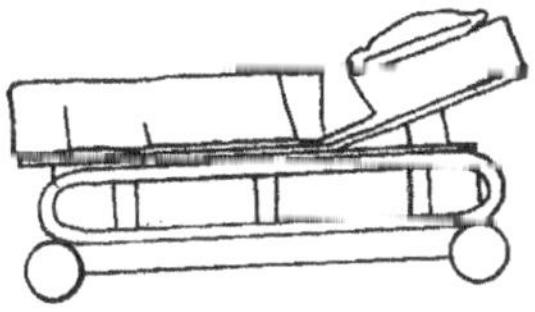

20)

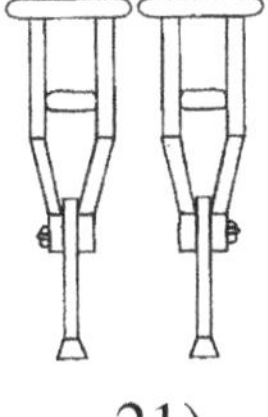

21)

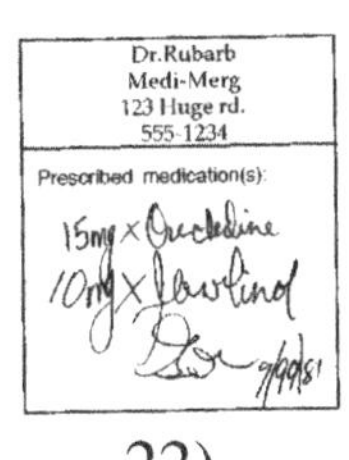
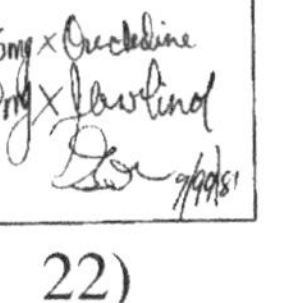

22)

23)

24)

ANSWER KEY

DRAWINGS Page 4

1) pills 2) stethoscope 3) bandage 4) surgeon 5) nurse 6) operation 7) prescription 8) surgical mask 9) stitches 10) cast 11) x ray 12) intravenous 13) crutches 14) reflexes 15) needle 16) doctor 17) sling 18) blood pressure 19) thermometer 20) hospital 21) emergency 22) hospital bed 23) wheelchair 24) rubber gloves

ORDERING

1) bandage 2) blood pressure 3) cast 4) crutches 5) doctor 6) emergency 7) hospital 8) hospital bed 9) intravenous 10) needle 11) nurse 12) operation 13) pills 14) prescription 15) reflexes 16) rubber gloves 17) sling 18) stethoscope 19) stitches 20) surgeon 21) surgical mask 22) thermometer 23) wheelchair 24) x ray

QUIZ

1) ?
2) pills, cast, sling, nurse
3) thermometer, intravenous, surgical mask, emergency, hospital bed, operation

DASHES

1) needle 2) surgeon 3) stethoscope 4) stitches 5) x ray 6) surgical mask 7) thermometer 8) wheelchair 9) blood pressure 10) pills 11) intravenous 12) prescription 13) bandage 14) hospital 15) rubber gloves 16) cast 17) emergency 18) hospital bed 19) crutches 20) doctor 21) operation 22) sling 23) nurse 24) reflexes

WORD SPIRAL

1) bandage 2) thermometer 3) x ray 4) operation 5) surgical mask 6) pills 7) wheelchair 8) hospital 9) nurse 10) stethoscope 11) cast 12) stitches 13) rubber gloves 14) blood pressure 15) needle 16) reflexes 17) surgeon 18) emergency 19) intravenous 20) hospital bed 21) crutches 22) prescription 23) sling 24) doctor

WORD MAZES

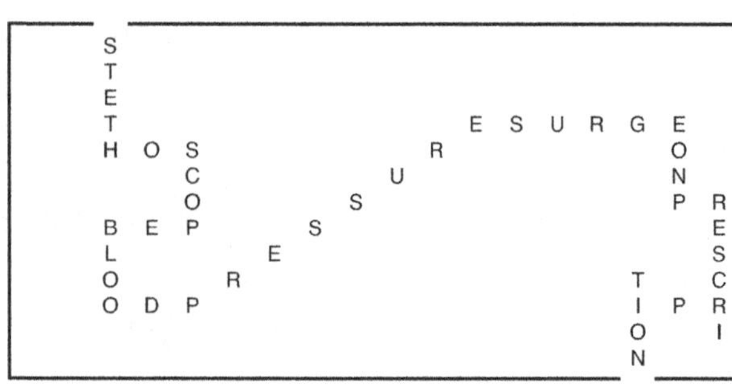

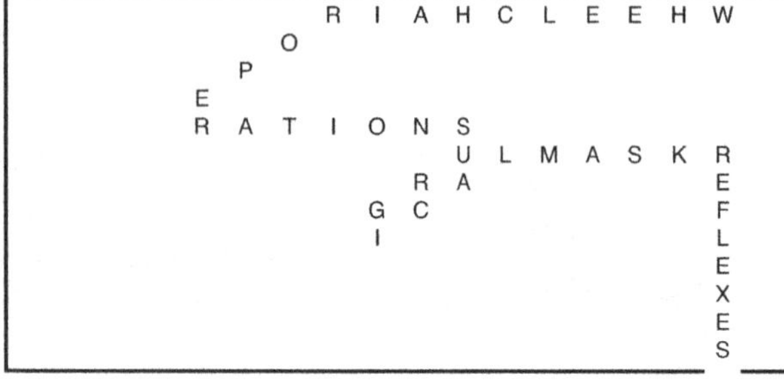

SCRAMBLES

1) examined 2) temperature

EIGHT MISTAKES

1) "I" from EXIT 2) bulb from lamp 3) "X" from X RAY 4) cord on intravenous 5) middle of small wheel on wheelchair 6) surgeon's hand 7) stripe on door handle 8) one rubber glove

FIND-THE-WORDS PUZZLE

```
R U B B E R G L O V E S     S I
    H   B A N D A G E       L N
O     C R U T C H E S   Y   I T
S       L A T I P S O H C T N R E
P R E S C R I P T I O N H G A R
I S E H C T I T S   E E E   V U
T         L S     P     G R   E S
A       L U   S O D   R M N N S
L     S R   E C   O E E O O E
B     G   X S A   C L M M I U R
E   E   E O   S   T D E E T S P
D O   L H     T   O E   T A N D
N   F T       R E   R U O
  E E         Y A R X N   R E R O
R T   W H E E L C H A I R P S L
S U R G I C A L M A S K   O E B
```

MAGIC WORD

1) stethoscope 2) prescription 3) emergency 4) needle 5) cast 6) doctor 7) hospital 8) intravenous 9) surgeon MAGIC WORD: spreading

CROSSWORD PUZZLE

ACROSS: 1) prescription 5) blood pressure 8) doctor 10) operation 15) cast 16) needle 20) surgeon 21) pills 22) hospital 23) emergency 24) sling DOWN: 2) thermometer 3) stethoscope 4) hospital bed 6) rubber gloves 7) surgical mask 9) x ray 11) intravenous 12) nurse 13) stitches 14) wheelchair 17) crutches 18) reflexes 19) bandage

TEST Page 13

1) bandage 2) thermometer 3) wheelchair 4) operation 5) surgical mask 6) pills 7) x ray 8) hospital 9) nurse 10) stethoscope 11) cast 12) stitches 13) rubber gloves 14) blood pressure 15) needle 16) reflexes 17) surgeon 18) emergency 19) intravenous 20) hospital bed 21) crutches 22) prescription 23) sling 24) doctor

Unit 6: Facial Expressions

SENTENCES

1. The young girls became hysterical when they saw the movie star.
2. My dad was disgusted when he saw my messy room.
3. Sad movies always make me cry.
4. The student became depressed after discovering that she failed her test.
5. I was shocked when I heard the bad news.
6. The newlywed couple looked rather amorous.
7. The mischievous kid jumped in the puddle and splashed his sister.
8. The stolen money was found in the guilty looking man's car.
9. I was quite embarrassed when my stomach rumbled at the dinner table.
10. I am overwhelmed by how much work I'm expected to do.
11. My mom was surprised when I washed the dishes without being asked.
12. My father was angry when I dented his car.
13. He did not study for the test and looked troubled as he wrote it.
14. The bride was anxious the night before her wedding.
15. The police arrested the suspicious looking man.
16. My uncle has been lonely ever since my aunt died.
17. I'm too frightened to ride roller coasters.
18. He looked a little timid because he was attending his first dance.
19. She was ecstatic when she won the lottery.
20. The audience looked pained as I began to sing.
21. I become bored while attending math class.
22. My girlfriend gets jealous whenever I talk to other girls.
23. She was exhausted after running the marathon race.
24. When a dog becomes happy, it will wag its tail.

6-3
1) hysterical
2) disgusted
3) sad
4) depressed
5) shocked
6) amorous
7) mischievous
8) guilty
9) embarrassed
10) overwhelmed
11) surprised
12) angry
13) troubled
14) anxious
15) suspicious
16) lonely
17) frightened
18) timid
19) ecstatic
20) pained
21) bored
22) jealous
23) exhausted
24) happy

1) lugtyi

2) mowledeevhr

3) guiseddts

4) aroomsu

5) ads

6) picissuuso

7) midit

8) riseupdrs

9) seedrepsd

10) sojulea

11) realyshtic

12) bledrout

13) veuchsosiim

14) rynag

15) elolyn

16) coshdek

17) cecistat

18) saxnoui

19) saxtheedu

20) raraseedmsb

21) ypaph

22) naipde

23) thendegrif

24) rodeb

ORDERING

Put the words in alphabetical order.

surprised	anxious	angry	amorous
happy	bored	frightened	lonely
guilty	troubled	exhausted	depressed
jealous	pained	ecstatic	overwhelmed
timid	sad	suspicious	mischievous
shocked	hysterical	embarrassed	disgusted

1) _______________________ 13) _______________________

2) _______________________ 14) _______________________

3) _______________________ 15) _______________________

4) _______________________ 16) _______________________

5) _______________________ 17) _______________________

6) _______________________ 18) _______________________

7) _______________________ 19) _______________________

8) _______________________ 20) _______________________

9) _______________________ 21) _______________________

10) _______________________ 22) _______________________

11) _______________________ 23) _______________________

12) _______________________ 24) _______________________

QUIZ

1) What word in the list is closest in meaning to the words a) sad and b) happy?

____

2) With a partner, one person makes a facial expression from the list and the other person guesses which one it is. Take turns.

____

3) Choose 6 facial expressions. Write a sentence for each explaining a situation when someone would wear that facial expression.

____

DASHES

Complete each word by adding the missing letters. Each dash represents a letter.

1) s _ _ p _ _ _ e d
2) t _ m _ _
3) h a _ _ y
4) s _ o _ k _ d
5) g _ _ l _ _
6) a n _ _ o _ _
7) j _ _ l _ _ s
8) e _ _ a _ _ t _ d
9) e _ b _ r _ a _ s e _
10) e _ _ t _ _ i _
11) a _ _ r _ _ s
12) s _ _ p _ _ i _ _ s
13) b _ _ _ _ d
14) h _ _ t _ r _ _ _ l
15) t _ o _ b _ e _
16) a _ _ r _
17) p a _ _ e _
18) f r _ _ h _ _ n _ _
19) s _ d
20) l o _ _ _ y
21) m _ _ c _ i _ _ o _ s
22) d _ _ r e _ _ e d
23) d i _ _ u _ _ _ d
24) o _ e _ w _ e _ m _ d

WORD SPIRAL

Following the spiral towards the center, circle all the vocabulary words from this unit.

anxiousdisgustedembarrassedguiltyamoroustimidangrylonelyjealousmischievousboreddepressedoverwhelmedexhaustedhystericalecstatichappysuspiciousfrightenedshockedsurprisedpainedsadtroubled

SCRAMBLES

Unscramble the jumbled letters to form words from this unit. Arrange the circled letters to form a surprise answer.

1

PUIDESRRS

CASTEITC

OLYENL

ANSWER: ___________________________

2

TUGLYI

SUROOMA

SOEHIMCSIVU

ANSWER: ___________________________

WORD MAZES

To find your way out of each maze, follow words from the unit from START to FINISH.
The words can go from left-to-right, from right-to-left, upward, downward or diagonally.

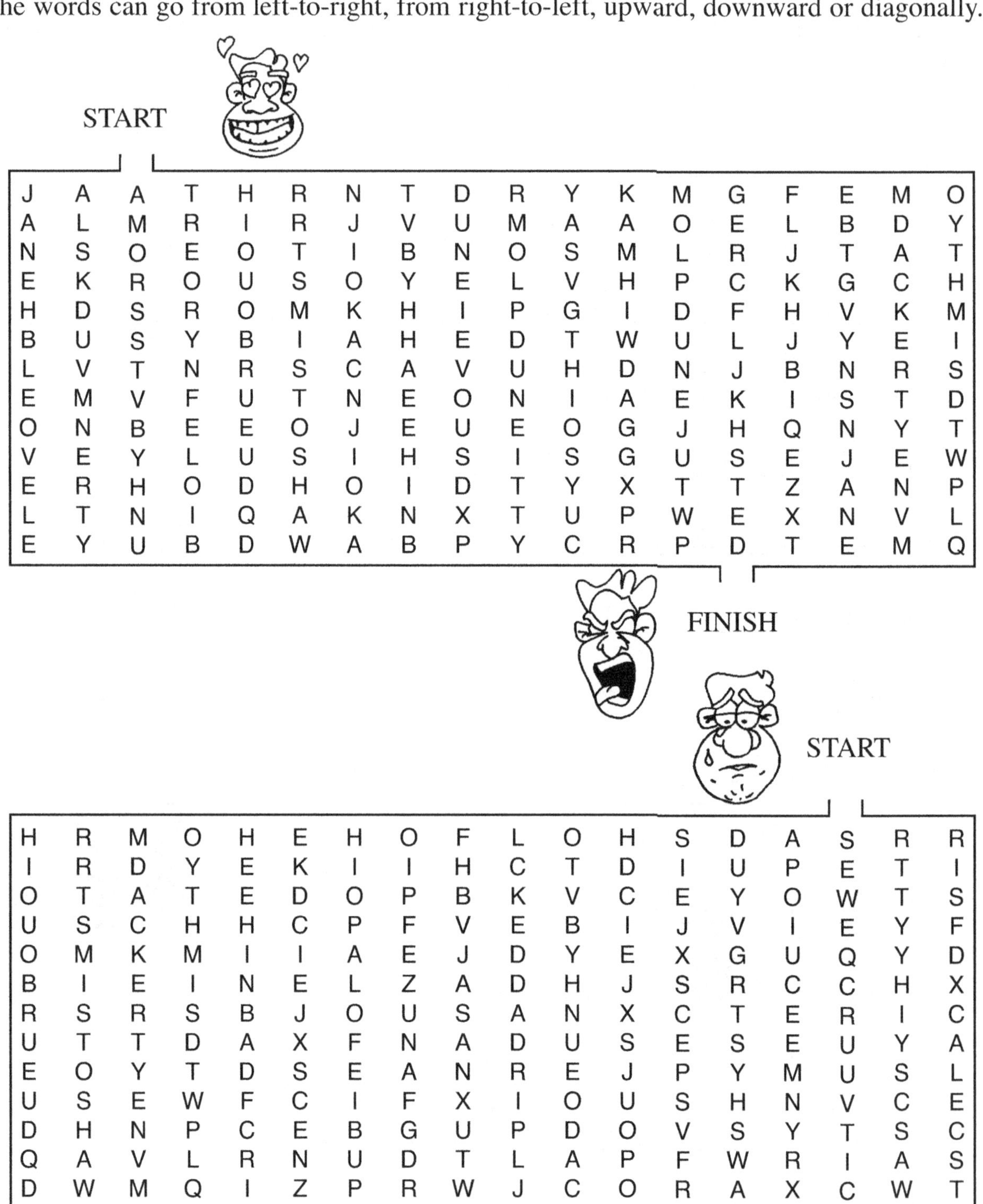

MAGIC WORD

Using words from the unit, complete the fill in the blanks exercise below. When you fill in those words on the chart an extra word will appear in the box.

1) ___ ___ ___ | ___ | ___ ___ ___ ___ ___ ___

2) ___ ___ ___ ___ | ___ ___ ___ ___ ___ ___

3) ___ ___ ___ | ___ ___ ___

4) ___ ___ | ___ ___ ___

5) ___ ___ ___ ___ ___ | ___ ___ ___

6) ___ ___ ___ ___ ___ | ___ ___

7) ___ ___ ___ ___ ___ | ___ ___

8) ___ | ___ ___ ___ ___ ___ ___ ___ ___ ___ ___

9) ___ ___ ___ ___ | ___ ___

10) ___ ___ ___ ___ ___ ___ | ___

1) The young girls became _______________________ when they saw the movie star.

2) I'm too _______________________ to ride roller coasters.

3) My uncle has been _______________________ ever since my aunt died.

4) He looked a little _______________________ because he was attending his first dance.

5) The student became _______________________ after discovering that she failed her test.

6) I was _______________________ when I heard the bad news.

7) He did not study for the test and looked _______________________ as he wrote it.

8) I am _______________________ by how much work I'm expected to do.

9) The audience looked _______________________ as I began to sing

10) My girlfriend gets _______________________ whenever I talk to other girls.

MAGIC WORD: _______________________

EIGHT MISTAKES

There are 8 things missing from Picture Two that can be found in Picture One. Find the missing items and write them down.

1 ____

2 ____

3 ____

4 ____

5 ____

6 ____

7 ____

8 ____

CROSSWORD PUZZLE

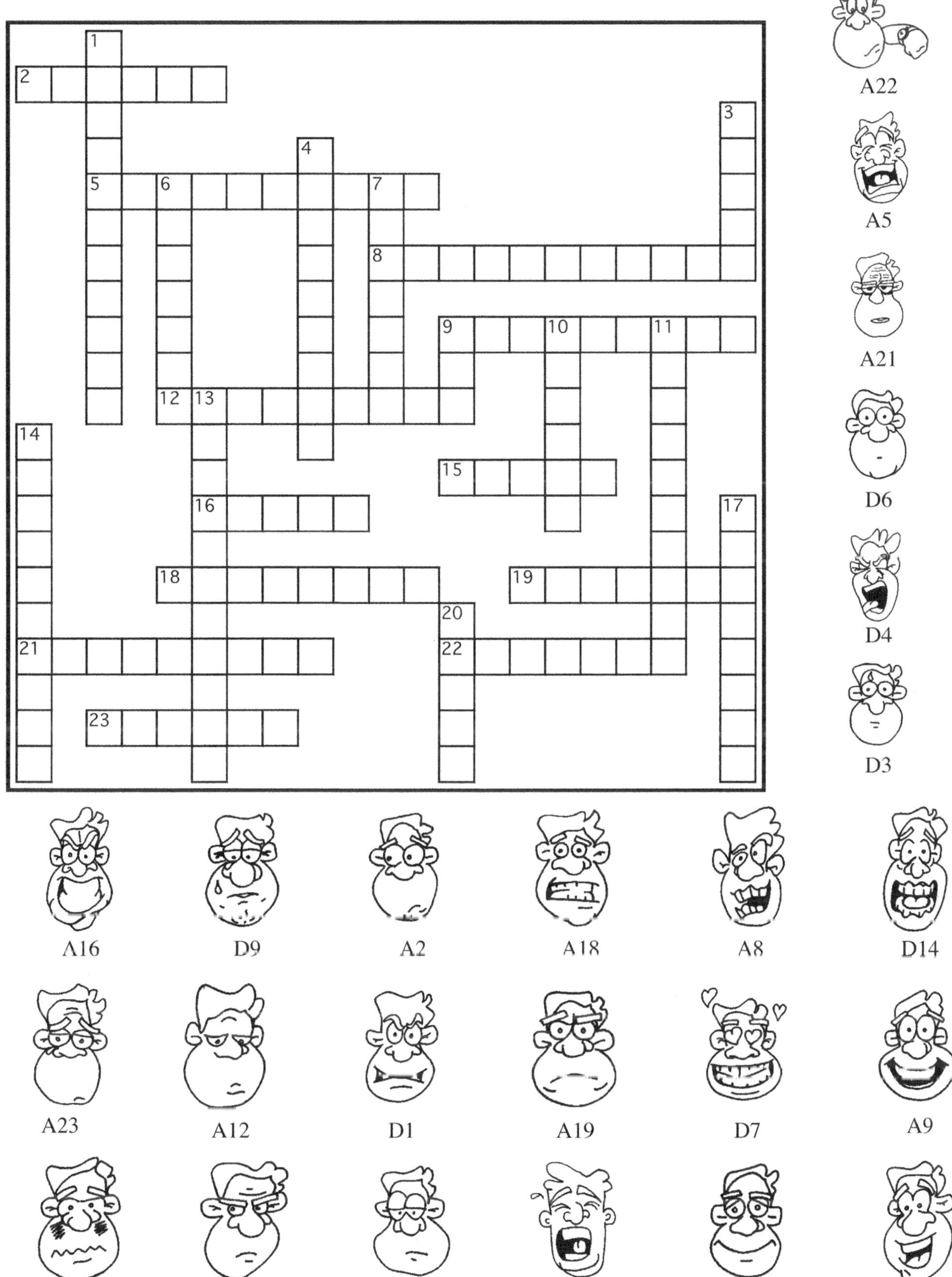

A22

A5

A21

D6

D4

D3

A16

D9

A2

A18

A8

D14

A23

A12

D1

A19

D7

A9

D13

D11

A15

D10

D20

D17

FIND-THE-WORDS PUZZLE

You will find all the words from this unit hidden in the box below. Find each word and circle all its letters. To find the words you may have to read from left-to-right, from right-to-left, upward, downward or diagonally.

```
Y  O  V  E  R  W  H  E  L  M  E  D  D  Q  J  M
R  E  P  P  A  M  O  R  O  U  S  J  S  S  E  I
G  R  O  D  E  S  I  R  P  R  U  S  A  U  A  S
N  L  P  N  T  U  H  X  N  M  W  H  S  S  L  C
A  A  D  E  T  S  U  G  S  I  D  O  D  P  O  H
B  C  C  H  L  I  G  C  E  D  D  C  E  I  U  I
A  I  S  W  A  O  F  V  C  E  F  K  S  C  S  E
D  R  E  E  Q  P  D  B  S  R  T  E  S  I  Y  V
E  E  M  D  W  P  P  S  T  O  I  D  E  O  U  O
T  T  J  E  E  O  A  Y  A  B  M  H  R  U  N  U
S  S  H  N  R  R  S  T  T  M  I  G  P  S  B  S
U  Y  T  I  R  L  A  L  I  L  D  H  E  C  A  G
A  H  R  A  T  K  Z  I  C  P  Y  F  D  R  O  D
H  L  B  P  Y  J  S  U  O  I  X  N  A  V  I  G
X  M  A  S  F  R  I  G  H  T  E  N  E  D  V  F
E  D  E  L  B  U  O  R  T  K  Y  L  E  N  O  L
```

AMOROUS	HYSTERICAL
ANGRY	JEALOUS
ANXIOUS	LONELY
BORED	MISCHIEVOUS
DEPRESSED	OVERWHELMED
DISGUSTED	PAINED
ECSTATIC	SAD
EMBARRASSED	SHOCKED
EXHAUSTED	SURPRISED
FRIGHTENED	SUSPICIOUS
GUILTY	TIMID
HAPPY	TROUBLED

1)
2)
3)
4)
5)
6)
7)
8)
9)
10)
11)
12)
13)
14)
15)
16)
17)
18)
19)
20)
21)
22)
23)
24)

ANSWER KEY

DRAWINGS Page 4

1) guilty 2) overwhelmed 3) disgusted 4) amorous 5) sad 6) suspicious 7) timid 8) surprised 9) depressed 10) jealous
11) hysterical 12) troubled 13) mischievous 14) angry 15) lonely 16) shocked 17) ecstatic 18) anxious 19) exhausted
20) embarrassed 21) happy 22) pained 23) frightened 24) bored

ORDERING

1) amorous 2) angry 3) anxious 4) bored 5) depressed 6) disgusted 7) ecstatic 8) embarrassed 9) exhausted 10) frightened
11) guilty 12) happy 13) hysterical 14) jealous 15) lonely 16) mischievous 17) overwhelmed 18) pained 19) sad 20) shocked
21) surprised 22) suspicious 23) timid 24) troubled

QUIZ

1) a) depressed   b) ecstatic
2) ?
3) ?

DASHES

1) surprised 2) timid 3) happy 4) shocked 5) guilty 6) anxious 7) jealous 8) exhausted 9) embarrassed 10) ecstatic 11) amorous
12) suspicious 13) bored 14) hysterical 15) troubled 16) angry 17) pained 18) frightened 19) sad 20) lonely 21) mischievous
22) depressed 23) disgusted 24) overwhelmed

WORD SPIRAL

1) anxious 2) disgusted 3) embarrassed 4) guilty 5) amorous 6) timid 7) angry 8) lonely 9) jealous 10) mischievous 11) bored
12) depressed 13) overwhelmed 14) exhausted 15) hysterical 16) ecstatic 17) happy 18) suspicious 19) frightened 20) shocked
21) sad 22) pained 23) surprised 24) troubled

WORD MAZES

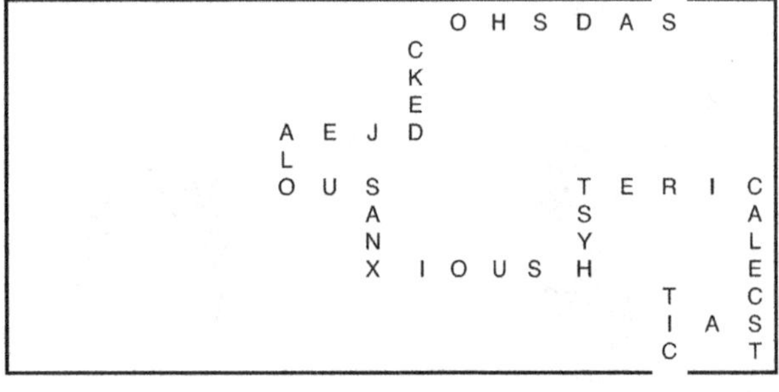

SCRAMBLES

1) audience 2) stomach

EIGHT MISTAKES

1) knot in tree 2) fire engine antenna 3) bird's tail
4) woman's eyebrow 5) dog's tail 6) headlight on fire engine
7) bottom rung of ladder 8) leaf at bottom of the tree

FIND-THE-WORDS PUZZLE

```
Y O V E R W H E L M E D     J M
R     A M O R O U S       S E I
G       D E S I R P R U S   U A S
N L               H       S L C
A A D E T S U G S   I D O D P O H
  C   H           E D D C E   I U I
  I       A       C E   K S C S E
D R           P   S R T E S I   V
E E   D       P S T O I D E O   O
T T   E     A Y A B M   R U   U
S S   N   R   T T   I   P S   S
U Y   I R     L I   D   E   A
A H   A       I C   D     D
H   B P     S U O I X N A
X M     F R I G H T E N E D
E D E L B U O R T   Y L E N O L
```

MAGIC WORD

1) hysterical 2) frightened 3) lonely 4) timid 5) depressed 6) shocked 7) troubled 8) overwhelmed 9) pained 10) jealous   MAGIC WORD: themselves

CROSSWORD PUZZLE

ACROSS: 2) guilty 5) hysterical 8) overwhelmed 9) surprised 12) depressed 15) bored 16) angry 18) troubled
19) jealous 21) exhaused 22) anxious 23) lonely   DOWN: 1) mischievous 3) timid 4) disgusted 6) shocked 7) amorous 9) sad
10) pained 11) suspicious 13) embarrassed 14) frightened 17) ecstatic 20) happy

TEST Page 13

1) anxious 2) disgusted 3) embarrassed 4) guilty 5) amorous 6) timid 7) angry 8) lonely 9) jealous 10) mischievous 11) bored
12) depressed 13) overwhelmed 14) exhausted 15) hysterical 16) ecstatic 17) happy 18) suspicious 19) frightened 20) shocked
21) sad 22) pained 23) surprised 24) troubled

Unit 7: Shapes & Math Terms

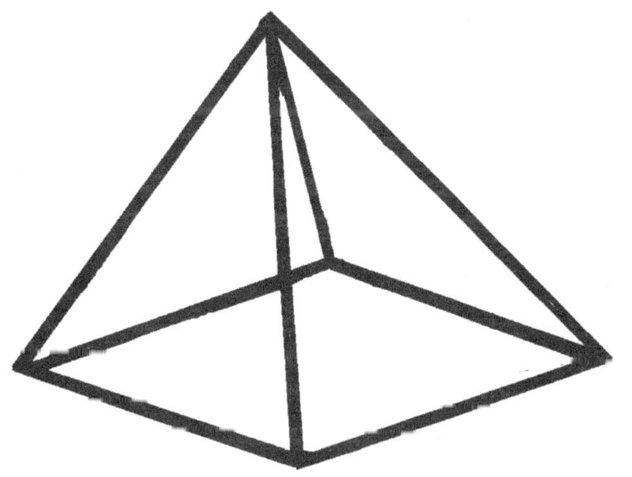

SENTENCES

1. If you multiply three and two, you get six.
2. Pennies are just a fraction of a dollar.
3. A stop sign is shaped like a polygon.
4. I had ice cream in a cone.
5. A can of soda is shaped like a cylinder.
6. A rectangle has two long equal sides, and two shorter equal sides.
7. A hexagon has six equal sides.
8. An egg is oval shaped.
9. A square has four sides that are equal in length.
10. If you add three plus two, you get five.
11. A globe of our planet is an example of a sphere.
12. Please divide that apple pie into six pieces.
13. Baseball is played on a field shaped like a diamond.
14. A trapezoid has four sides only two of which are parallel.
15. When I vacationed in Egypt, I saw a pyramid.
16. As a decimal, one quarter is written as 0.25.
17. A triangle has three sides.
18. The prism in the drawing is a rectangular prism.
19. Dice are cube shaped.
20. If you subtract two from three, you get one.
21. Sometimes the moon looks crescent shaped.
22. The buttons on my shirt are round.
23. There was a heart on her Valentine's Day card.
24. One hundred pennies equals one dollar.

7 3

1) multiply

2) fraction

3) polygon

4) cone

5) cylinder

6) rectangle

7) hexagon

8) oval

9) square

10) add

11) sphere

12) divide

13) diamond

14) trapezoid

15) pyramid

16) decimal

17) triangle

18) prism

19) cube

20) subtract

21) crescent

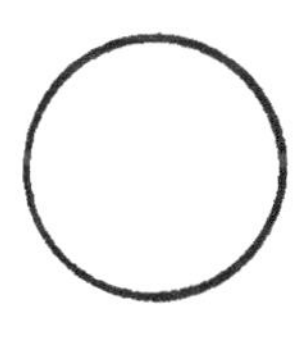

22) round

23) heart

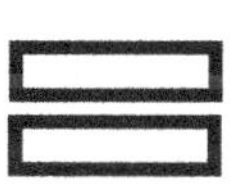

24) equals

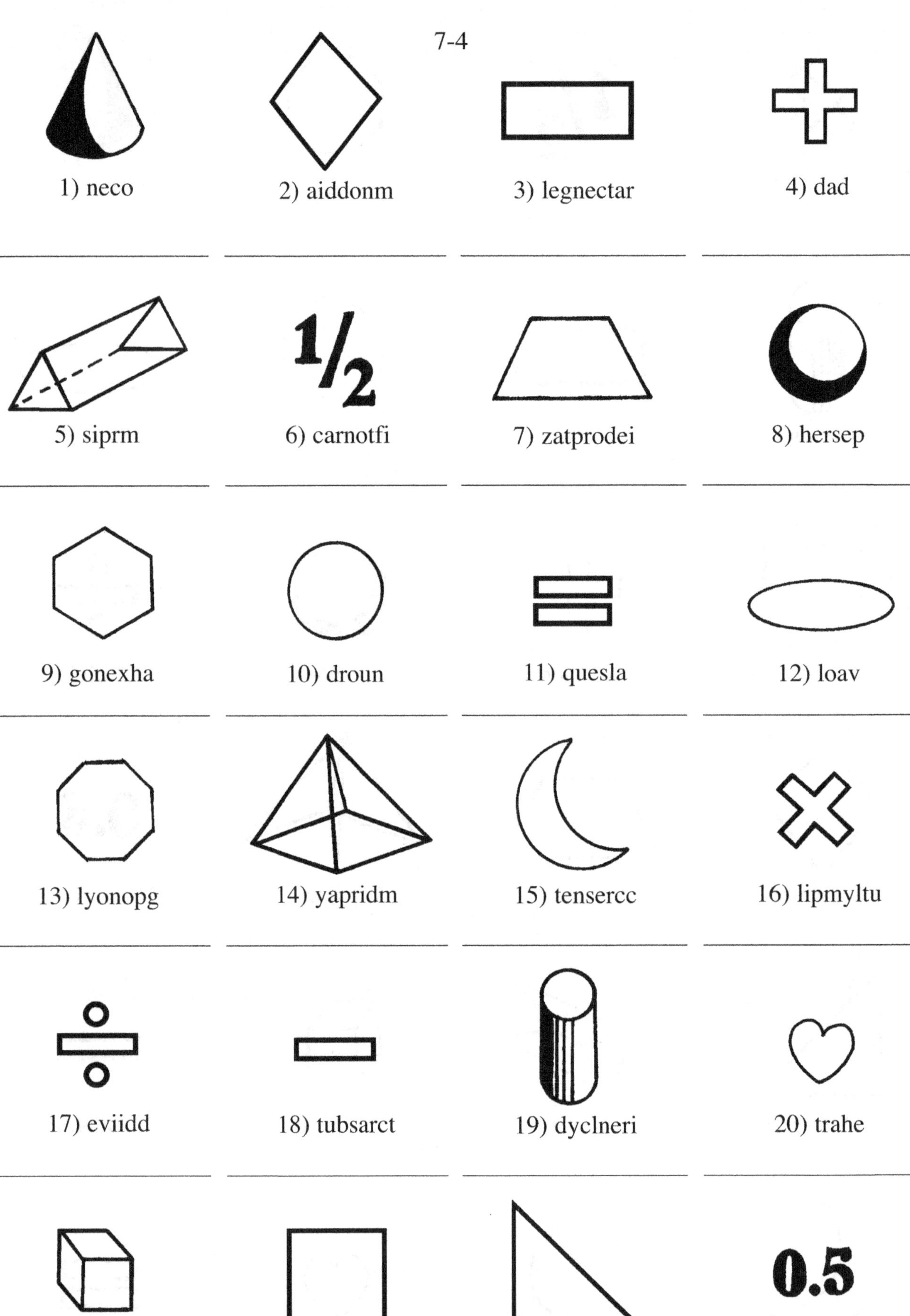

1) neco
2) aiddonm
3) legnectar
4) dad
5) siprm
6) carnotfi
7) zatprodei
8) hersep
9) gonexha
10) droun
11) quesla
12) loav
13) lyonopg
14) yapridm
15) tensercc
16) lipmyltu
17) eviidd
18) tubsarct
19) dyclneri
20) trahe
21) buec
22) raqeus
23) leangrit
24) calmedi

ORDERING

Put the words in alphabetical order.

triangle	divide	oval	round
polygon	fraction	prism	sphere
crescent	heart	square	subtract
cylinder	decimal	pyramid	add
trapezoid	multiply	hexagon	cone
diamond	cube	rectangle	equals

1) _______________________   13) _______________________

2) _______________________   14) _______________________

3) _______________________   15) _______________________

4) _______________________   16) _______________________

5) _______________________   17) _______________________

6) _______________________   18) _______________________

7) _______________________   19) _______________________

8) _______________________   20) _______________________

9) _______________________   21) _______________________

10) _______________________   22) _______________________

11) _______________________   23) _______________________

12) _______________________   24) _______________________

QUIZ

1) Make 2 lists. Make a list of all the shapes in the unit. And make a different list of all the math terms in the unit.

____

2) Look around the room. Do you see any objects that are shaped like the shapes mentioned in this unit? Identify the object and the shape.

____

3) Using only the shapes in the list, draw a picture of a face. Try to use as many of the shapes as possible.

____

DASHES

Complete each word by adding the missing letters. Each dash represents a letter.

1) a _ _
2) d _ c _ m _ _
3) s _ _ t _ _ _ t
4) r _ u _ d
5) d _ _ i _ _
6) s _ u _ _ e
7) e _ u _ _ s
8) d _ _ m _ _ d
9) m _ l _ i _ _ y
10) r e _ _ a _ _ _ e
11) f _ _ c _ i _ n
12) c _ _ s _ _ n t

13) t r _ _ n _ _ e
14) h e _ _ g _ _
15) o _ _ l
16) p _ i _ _
17) c _ _ i _ _ e r
18) h _ _ _ t
19) c u _ _
20) s _ _ e _ e
21) p _ _ a m _ _
22) t _ _ p _ _ o _ d
23) p _ _ _ g _ n
24) c _ n _

WORD SPIRAL

Following the spiral towards the center, circle all the vocabulary words from this unit.

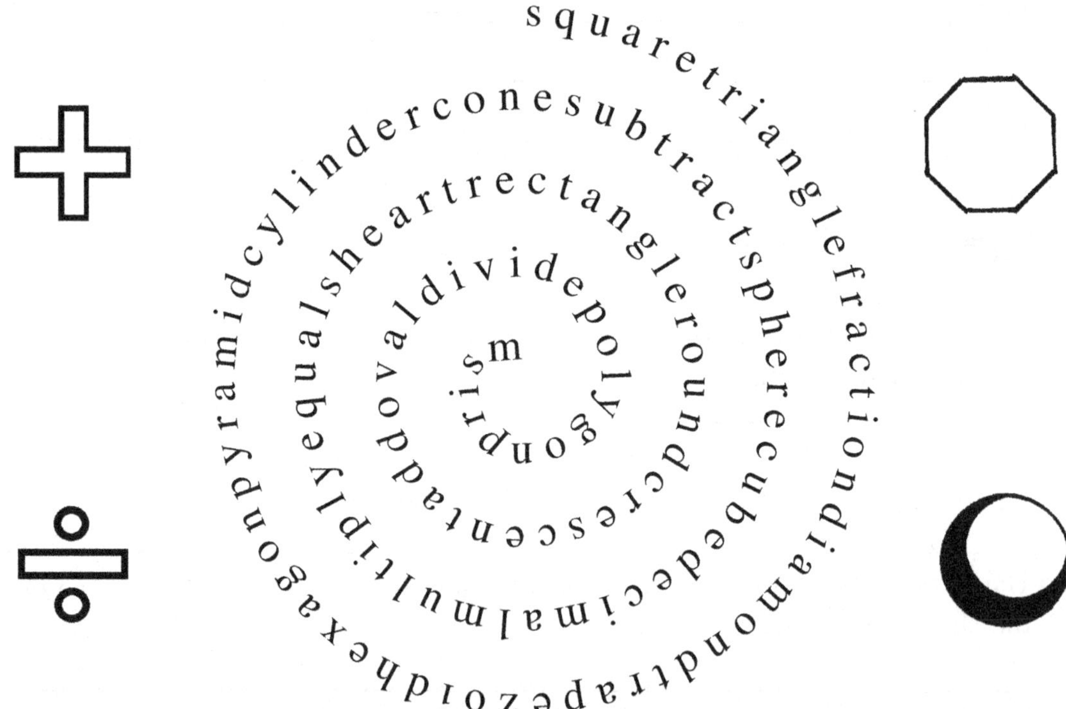

SCRAMBLES

Unscramble the jumbled letters to form words from this unit. Arrange the circled letters to form a surprise answer.

1

ERATH

DRUNO

DIEVDI

ANSWER: ____

2

DRYCLINE

NYLOOPG

HEEPSR

ANSWER: ____

WORD MAZES

To find your way out of each maze, follow words from the unit from START to FINISH. The words can go from left-to-right, from right-to-left, upward, downward or diagonally.

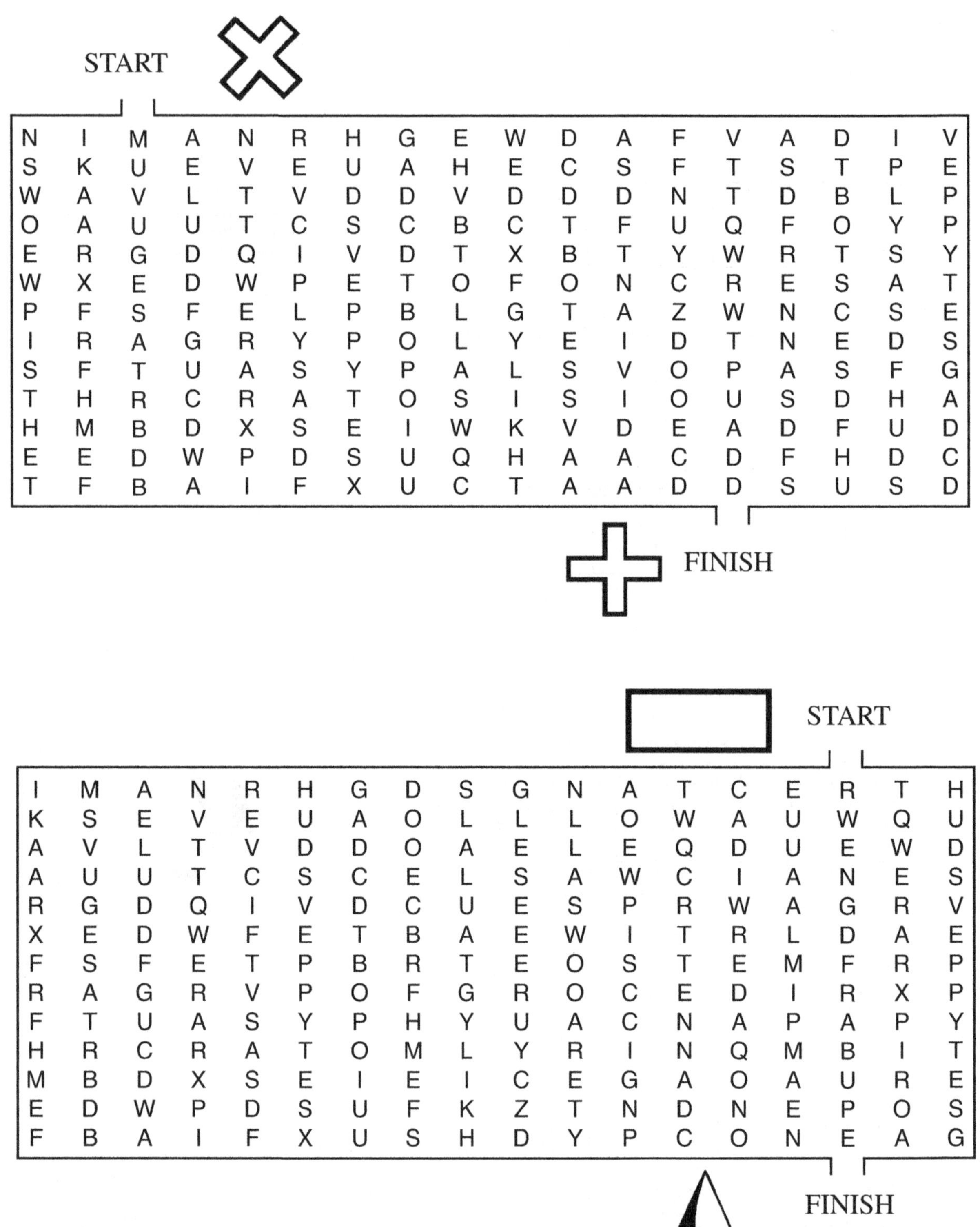

MAGIC WORD

Using words from the unit, complete the fill in the blanks exercise below. When you fill in those words on the chart an extra word will appear in the box.

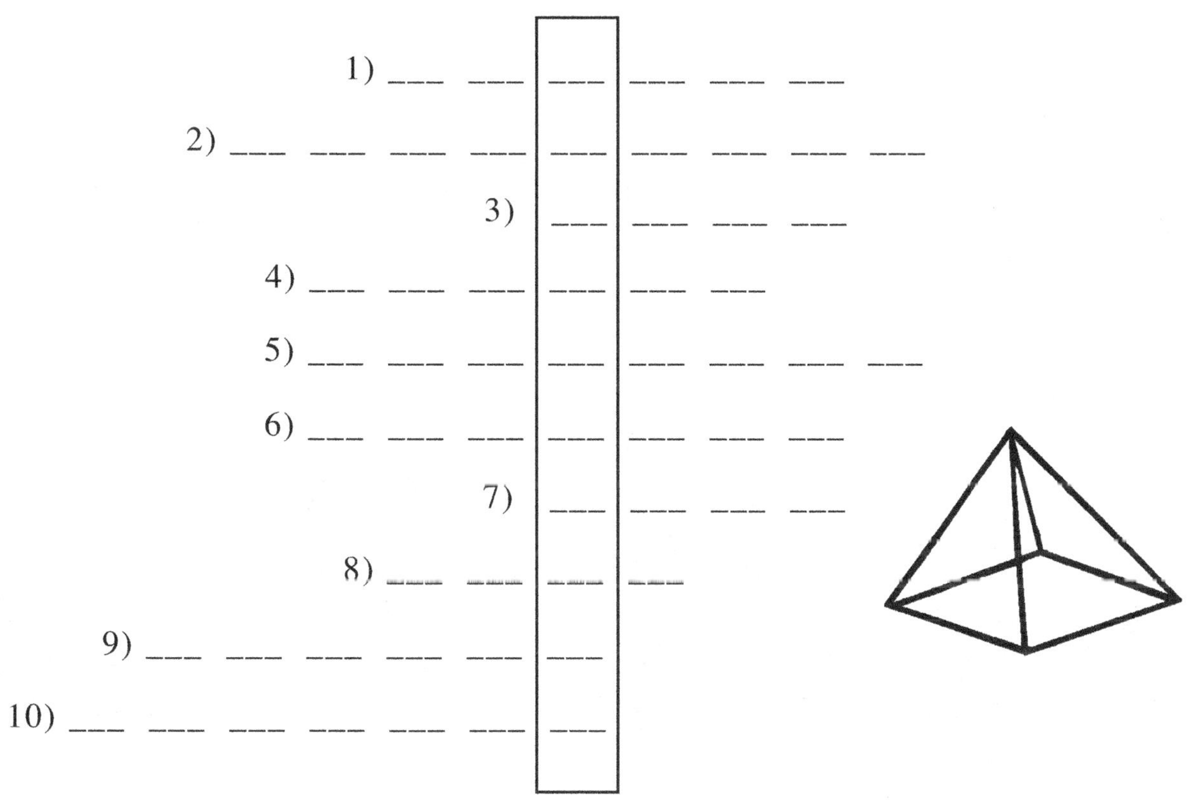

1) ___ ___ | ___ ___ ___ ___

2) ___ ___ ___ ___ | ___ ___ ___ ___ ___

3) ___ | ___ ___ ___

4) ___ ___ ___ | ___ ___ ___

5) ___ ___ ___ | ___ ___ ___ ___

6) ___ ___ ___ | ___ ___ ___ ___

7) ___ | ___ ___ ___

8) ___ ___ | ___ ___

9) ___ ___ ___ ___ ___ ___

10) ___ ___ ___ ___ ___ ___ ___

1) Please _______________________ that apple pie into six pieces.

2) A _______________________ has two long equal sides, and two shorter equal sides.

3) Dice are _______________________ shaped.

4) A _______________________ has four sides that are equal in length.

5) If you _______________________ two from three, you get one.

6) As a _______________________, one quarter is written as 0.25.

7) An egg is _______________________ shaped.

8) I had ice cream in a _______________________.

9) A globe of our planet is an example of a _______________________.

10) Baseball is played on a field shaped like a _______________________.

MAGIC WORD: _______________________

EIGHT MISTAKES

There are 8 things missing from Picture Two that can be found in Picture One. Find the missing items and write them down.

1 ____

2 ____

3 ____

4 ____

5 ____

6 ____

7 ____

8 ____

CROSSWORD PUZZLE

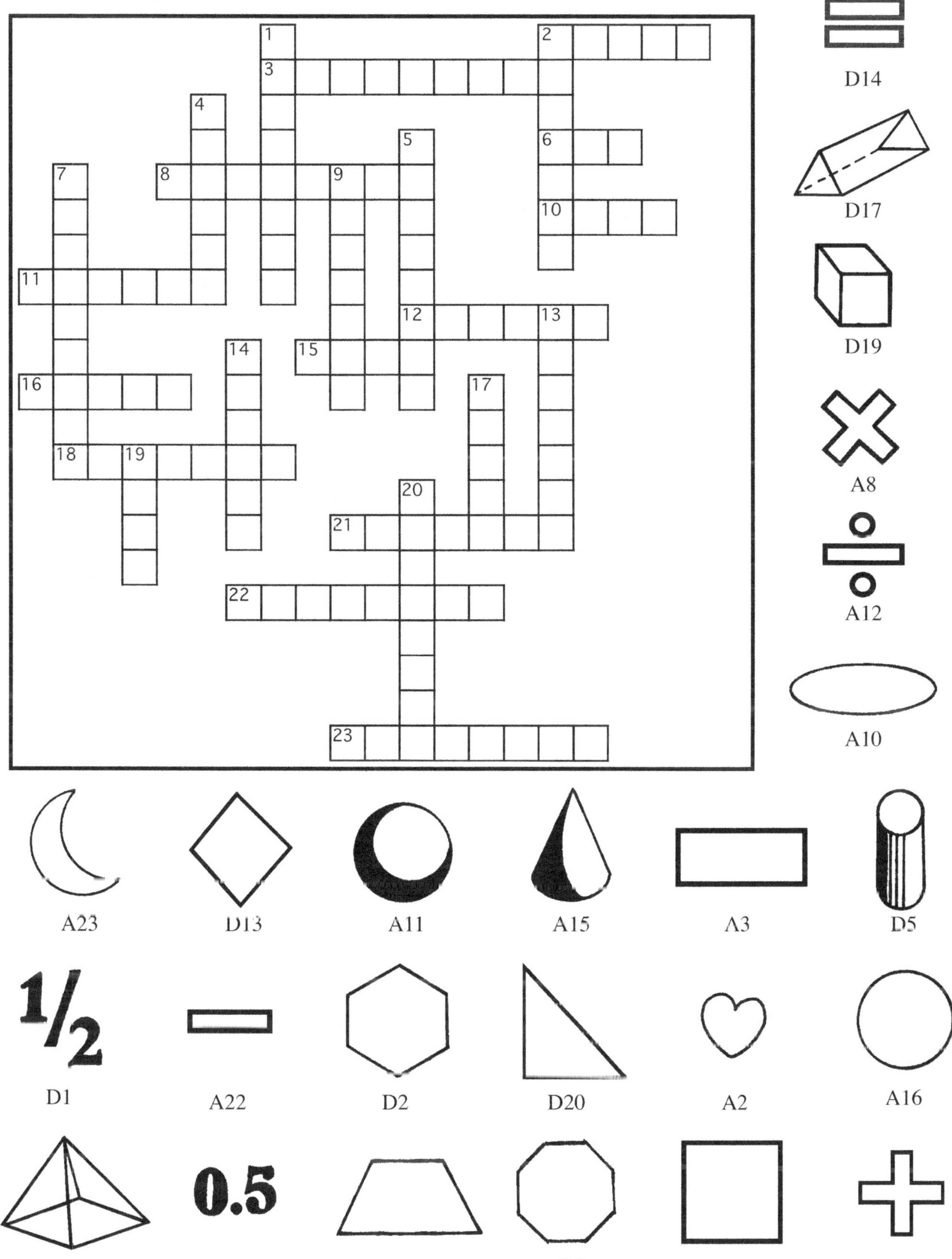

FIND-THE-WORDS PUZZLE

You will find all the words from this unit hidden in the box below. Find each word and circle all its letters. To find the words you may have to read from left-to-right, from right-to-left, upward, downward or diagonally.

```
R  C  Y  L  I  N  D  E  R  C  E  R  A  U  Q  S
E  S  S  P  Q  R  S  M  C  H  D  N  S  M  X  P
C  G  U  O  C  U  B  E  C  O  N  E  F  O  R  H
T  Y  B  G  A  B  L  A  R  E  O  N  H  L  O  E
A  B  T  D  D  D  A  R  E  S  M  I  J  S  U  R
N  J  R  C  U  W  M  B  S  T  A  N  Y  O  N  E
G  I  A  E  T  A  I  R  C  A  I  G  K  A  D  A
L  N  C  N  E  I  C  E  E  T  D  E  Y  I  B  J
E  O  T  O  D  V  E  L  N  E  Q  S  O  O  U  N
H  G  C  I  S  E  D  G  T  S  W  Z  T  K  D  O
E  A  N  T  X  I  H  N  L  P  E  R  Y  H  V  G
L  X  B  C  M  E  G  A  S  P  O  F  T  A  T  Y
Z  E  E  A  A  A  U  I  A  L  V  V  L  J  A  L
M  H  R  R  A  Q  A  R  I  E  D  I  V  I  D  O
O  Y  T  F  E  T  T  T  K  A  L  S  D  O  G  P
P  R  I  S  M  O  O  Y  L  P  I  T  L  U  M  A
```

ADD	MULTIPLY
CONE	OVAL
CRESCENT	POLYGON
CUBE	PRISM
CYLINDER	PYRAMID
DECIMAL	RECTANGLE
DIAMOND	ROUND
DIVIDE	SPHERE
EQUALS	SQUARE
FRACTION	SUBTRACT
HEART	TRAPEZOID
HEXAGON	TRIANGLE

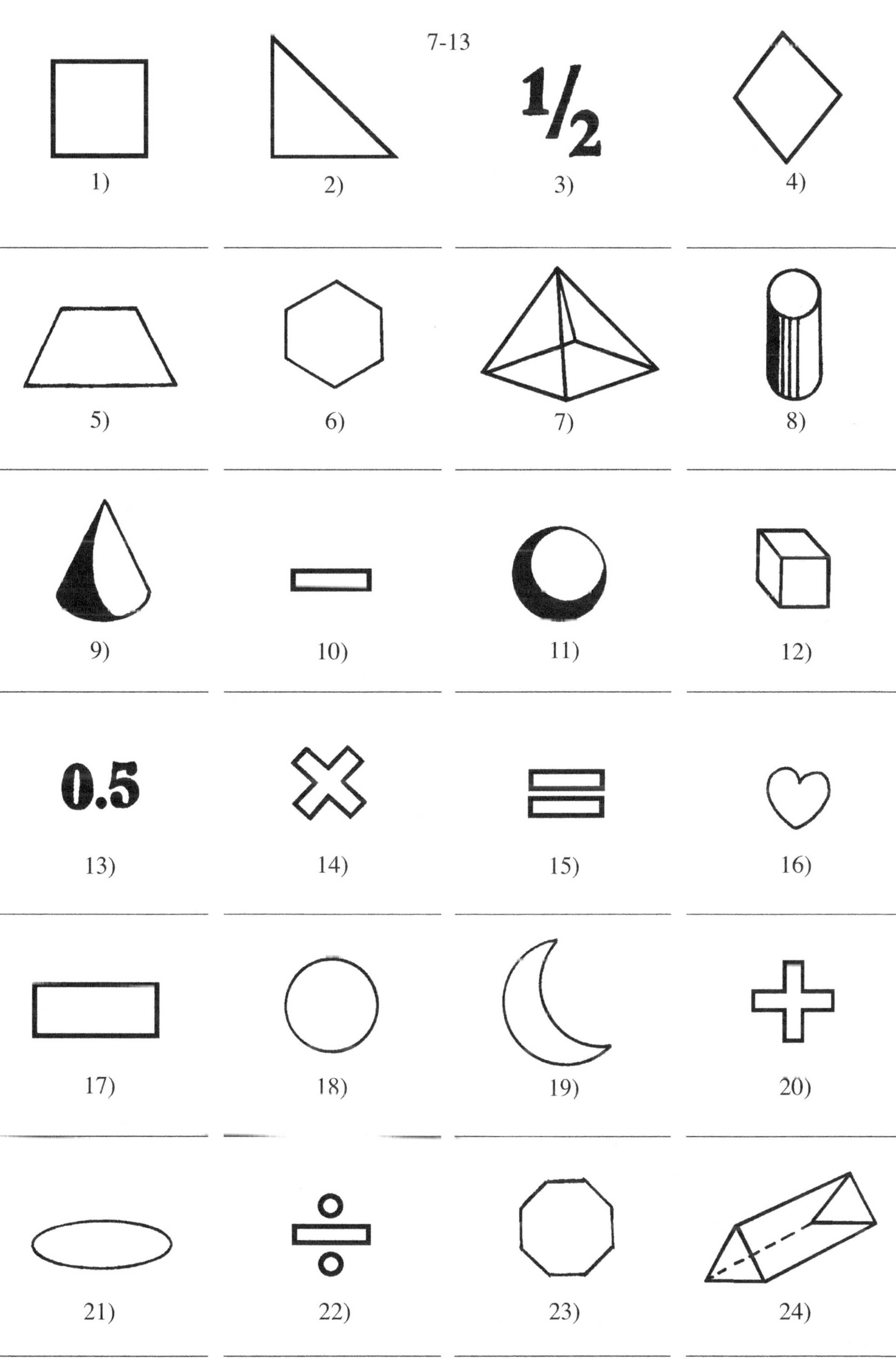

ANSWER KEY

DRAWINGS Page 4

1) cone 2) diamond 3) rectangle 4) add 5) prism 6) fraction 7) trapezoid 8) sphere 9) hexagon 10) round 11) equals 12) oval 13) polygon 14) pyramid 15) crescent 16) multiply 17) divide 18) subtract 19) cylinder 20) heart 21) cube 22) square 23) triangle 24) decimal

ORDERING

1) add 2) cone 3) crescent 4) cube 5) cylinder 6) decimal 7) diamond 8) divide 9) equals 10) fraction 11) heart 12) hexagon 13) multiply 14) oval 15) polygon 16) prism 17) pyramid 18) rectangle 19) round 20) sphere 21) square 22) subtract 23) trapezoid 24) triangle

QUIZ

1) Shapes: cone, crescent, cube, cylinder, diamond, heart, hexagon, oval, polygon, prism, pyramid, rectangle, round, sphere, square, trapezoid, triangle Math Terms: add, decimal, divide, equals, fraction, multiply, subtract
2) ? 3) ?

DASHES

1) add 2) decimal 3) subtract 4) round 5) divide 6) square 7) equals 8) diamond 9) multiply 10) rectangle 11) fraction 12) crescent 13) triangle 14) hexagon 15) oval 16) prism 17) cylinder 18) heart 19) cube 20) sphere 21) pyramid 22) trapezoid 23) polygon 24) cube

WORD SPIRAL

1) square 2) triangle 3) fraction 4) diamond 5) trapezoid 6) hexagon 7) pyramid 8) cylinder 9) cone 10) subtract 11) sphere 12) cube 13) decimal 14) multiply 15) equals 16) heart 17) rectangle 18) round 19) crescent 20) add 21) oval 22) divide 23) polygon 24) prism

WORD MAZES

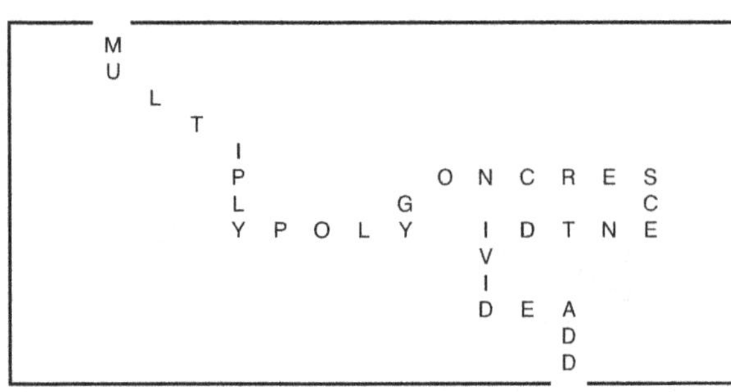

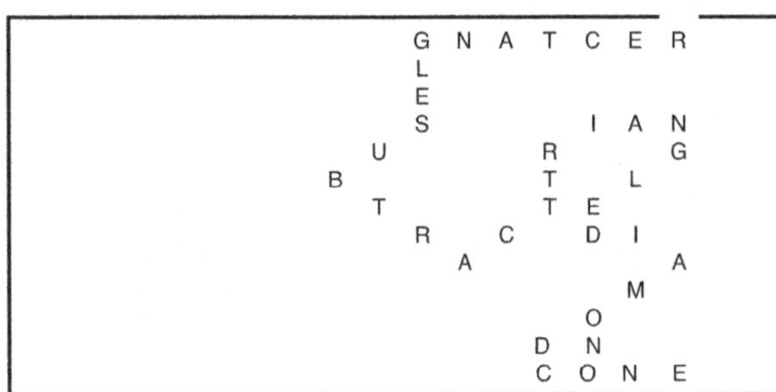

SCRAMBLES

1) hundred 2) pennies

EIGHT MISTAKES

1) left heart on wagon 2) piece of twig sticking out of snowman 3) block of snow beneath person at igloo 4) one of the sun's eyes 5) top of igloo 6) snow at base of snowman 7) hand of boy building snowman 8) fringes on boy's scarf

FIND-THE-WORDS PUZZLE

R	C	Y	L	I	N	D	E	R		E	R	A	U	Q	S
E		S						D							P
C		U		C	U	B	E	C	O	N	E		R	H	
T		B			L		R	O				O		E	
A		T	D	D	A		E	M				U	R		
N		R			M		S	A				N	D		
G		A			I		C	I				D			
L	N	C	N		C	E	E	D			I				
E	O	T	O		E	L	N			O			N		
	G		I		D	G	T	S		Z			O		
	A		T	I	H	N	L		E			V	G		
	X		C	M	E	A		P			A		Y		
	E		A	A	U	I	A			L		L			
	H	R	R	Q	R		E	D	I	V	I	D	O		
	Y	T	F	E	T	T							P		
P	R	I	S	M		Y	L	P	I	T	L	U	M		

MAGIC WORD

1) divide 2) rectangle 3) cube 4) square 5) subtract 6) decimal 7) oval 8) cone 9) sphere 10) diamond   MAGIC WORD: vacationed

CROSSWORD PUZZLE

ACROSS: 2) heart 3) rectangle 6) add 8) multiply 10) oval 11) sphere 12) divide 15) cone 16) round 18) decimal 21) pyramid 22) subtract 23) crescent   DOWN: 1) fraction 2) hexagon 4) square 5) cylinder 7) trapezoid 9) polygon 13) diamond 14) equals 17) prism 19) cube 20) triangle

TEST Page 13

1) square 2) triangle 3) fraction 4) diamond 5) trapezoid 6) hexagon 7) pyramid 8) cylinder 9) cone 10) subtract 11) sphere 12) cube 13) decimal 14) multiply 15) equals 16) heart 17) rectangle 18) round 19) crescent 20) add 21) oval 22) divide 23) polygon 24) prism

Unit 8: Verbs of Action

SENTENCES

1. A good exercise is to bend over and touch your toes.
2. I always sing in the shower.
3. Jimmy liked to hop over puddles.
4. I am too weak to open the jar.
5. I ride my bike to school every day.
6. Horror movies make her scream.
7. My baby sister is always trying to bite me.
8. I enjoy going to the park because I get to slide very fast.
9. You should always stretch your muscles before you exercise.
10. I got to blow out the candles on my birthday cake.
11. Our car ran out of gas, so we had to push it to the gas station.
12. My nephew likes to swing at the park.
13. He tried to pull the rope as hard as he could.
14. When my mom makes chocolate cake, she lets me stir the ingredients.
15. I saw that girl wink at me.
16. Please do not slam the drawer when you close it.
17. She liked to brush her hair before going to bed.
18. He began to wave when he saw his friends approaching.
19. She loves to play tennis.
20. I always whistle when I work.
21. The bride and groom gave each other a kiss on their wedding day.
22. She loved to skip rope.
23. Someone might fall if you leave your toys on the stairs.
24. When you have an itch, you scratch it.

1) bend

2) sing

3) hop

4) open

5) ride

6) scream

7) bite

8) slide

9) stretch

10) blow

11) push

12) swing

13) pull

14) stir

15) wink

16) close

17) brush

18) wave

19) play

20) whistle

21) kiss

22) skip

23) fall

24) scratch

1) chartsc

2) lafl

3) sisk

4) ginsw

5) pisk

6) lsewhit

7) phsu

8) elsdi

9) ullp

10) oblw

11) teib

12) pone

13) chetstr

14) seramc

15) ohp

16) subhr

17) eidr

18) gins

19) celso

20) ylpa

21) dbne

22) kiwn

23) wvea

24) irts

ORDERING

Put the words in alphabetical order.

hop	slide	pull	open
skip	brush	push	close
ride	stir	scream	play
sing	whistle	fall	bite
bend	scratch	stretch	wave
swing	wink	blow	kiss

1) _______________________

2) _______________________

3) _______________________

4) _______________________

5) _______________________

6) _______________________

7) _______________________

8) _______________________

9) _______________________

10) _______________________

11) _______________________

12) _______________________

13) _______________________

14) _______________________

15) _______________________

16) _______________________

17) _______________________

18) _______________________

19) _______________________

20) _______________________

21) _______________________

22) _______________________

23) _______________________

24) _______________________

QUIZ

1) What verb is the opposite of a) push? b) close?

____

2) With a partner, one person act out one of the verbs and the other person respond by naming it. Take turns.

____

3) List all of the verbs that describe what you did today.

____

DASHES

Complete each word by adding the missing letters. Each dash represents a letter.

1) h _ _

2) s _ _ r

3) s _ _ p

4) w _ _ s _ _ e

5) r _ _ e

6) s _ _ a _ _ h

7) s i _ _

8) p _ _ l

9) s _ _ d _

10) p _ s _

11) b r _ _ _

12) w _ _ k

13) s _ _ e _ _

14) p _ _ y

15) f _ l _

16) b _ _ e

17) s t _ _ t _ _

18) w _ _ e

19) b _ _ w

20) k _ s _

21) o _ _ n

22) b e _ _

23) c l _ _ e

24) s _ _ n _

WORD SPIRAL

Following the spiral towards the center, circle all the vocabulary words from this unit.

SCRAMBLES

Unscramble the jumbled letters to form words from this unit. Arrange the circled letters to form a surprise answer.

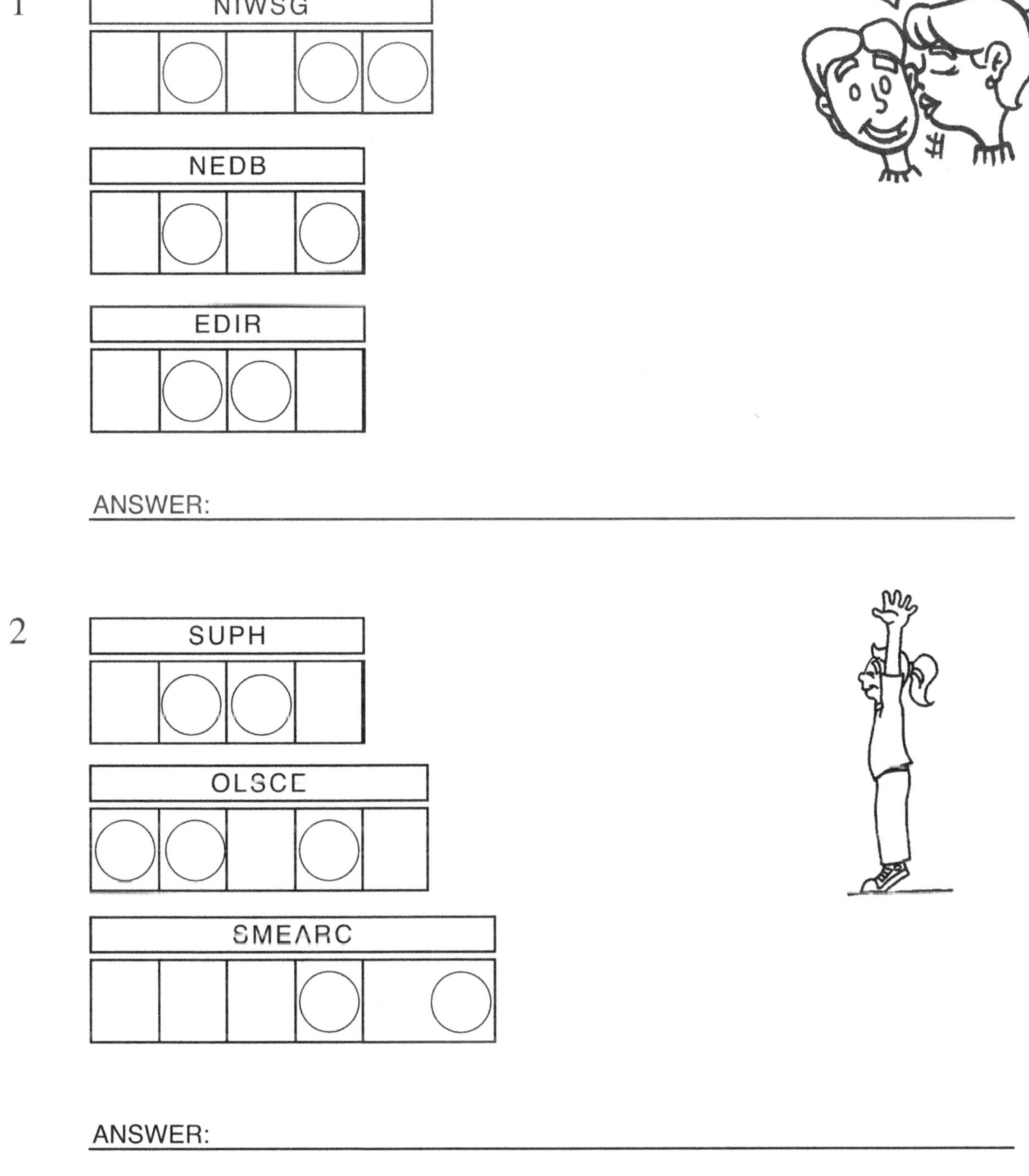

1

NIWSG

NEDB

EDIR

ANSWER: _______________________________

2

SUPH

OLSCE

SMEARC

ANSWER: _______________________________

WORD MAZES

To find your way out of each maze, follow words from the unit from START to FINISH.
The words can go from left-to-right, from right-to-left, upward, downward or diagonally.

START

```
L D W H I S G O E J E U D M R I M M
D D E T I T V S W Z R E R I C R B P
I G K P P L Y H E S H S F S T P G L
O V A U F E P L A Y B B H D K A H J
B D C I H J T I K I L M O T R N Y Z
R S T F U Z U R G R O U Y W I I T S
U R C G V S R P P W E Q T P S E U E
E Y O D E E W A O W B W H L T L R V
U T I R S V E N L A U E M Q L P W E
D H P F Y E R I I T V R B R D L W A
Q G W H U E R E M U I E Y U A I R E
D D E B G B T L P R A F T S N L R Y
B U C V T T T T L W O G H H K H T U
```

FINISH

START

```
H I S G T P S L I I A G K F A S O T
T I T V Y K E D R P C E A H N C S Y
P P L Y Y H K I P F K A M B I R H Y
U F E P A F A O A N I S H C T A L A
I H J T S S C B G A O H Y E E D I S
F U Z U V S T R G C I N T L L D R V
G V S R G T C U E N L U H P P G P G
D E E W T V O E R J A O M L L V R T
R S V E H B I U C A S R B I I L W H
F Y E R I Y P D F N E H O P S L E I
H U E R O H W Q L E P Y G I A I R O
B G B T P N E D J M M U D R T D R P
V T T T O U C B K D I C R P U E T O
```

START

FINISH

MAGIC WORD

Using words from the unit, complete the fill in the blanks exercise below. When you fill in those words on the chart an extra word will appear in the box.

1) ___ ___ | ___ | ___ ___

2) ___ ___ | ___ | ___

3) ___ ___ ___ ___ | ___

4) ___ ___ | ___ | ___ ___ ___

5) ___ ___ ___ | ___

6) ___ ___ ___ | ___

7) ___ | ___ | ___ ___

8) ___ ___ | ___ | ___

9) ___ ___ | ___ | ___

10) ___ ___ ___ ___ | ___ | ___ ___

11) ___ ___ ___ | ___ | ___

1) I enjoy going to the park because I get to _____________________ very fast.

2) I saw that girl _____________________ at me.

3) My nephew likes to _____________________ at the park.

4) Horror movies make her _____________________.

5) I _____________________ my bike to school every day.

6) A good exercise is to _____________________ over and touch your toes.

7) My baby sister is always trying to _____________________ me.

8) I am too weak to _____________________ the jar.

9) I always _____________________ in the shower.

10) I always _____________________ when I work.

11) She liked to _____________________ her hair before going to bed.

MAGIC WORD: _____________________

EIGHT MISTAKES

There are 8 things missing from Picture Two that can be found in Picture One. Find the missing items and write them down.

1 ____

2 ____

3 ____

4 ____

5 ____

6 ____

7 ____

8 ____

CROSSWORD PUZZLE

D8

A6

A12

A5

D3

D11

A18

A14

A9

D4

A19

D6

A7

D17

D18

A10

A17

A13

A15

D9

A3

D2

D16

A1

FIND-THE-WORDS PUZZLE

You will find all the words from this unit hidden in the box below. Find each word and circle all its letters. To find the words you may have to read from left-to-right, from right-to-left, upward, downward or diagonally.

```
I  U  A  N  X  E  S  S  R  I  D  E  N  N  E  G
C  G  S  L  I  D  E  T  O  T  G  E  U  U  T  N
L  B  L  T  U  U  J  V  S  Y  V  L  G  M  Y  I
O  D  K  B  N  T  H  C  T  E  R  T  S  O  T  S
S  E  I  F  Y  J  U  R  I  C  T  B  E  P  H  T
E  C  N  E  T  P  K  T  R  D  O  T  L  E  R  O
T  R  T  C  R  O  N  Y  I  W  D  A  N  N  E  P
H  B  R  U  S  H  I  U  B  E  Y  R  T  B  I  U
I  V  H  A  P  Q  W  O  L  B  M  O  S  E  N  S
P  U  L  L  O  W  H  S  S  E  A  C  B  R  H  H
N  E  E  L  D  C  K  W  S  N  L  H  R  I  A  N
K  T  R  L  T  X  I  E  A  D  R  T  E  N  T  N
I  O  A  A  A  N  M  A  C  U  C  U  S  I  M  E
L  W  R  F  G  S  D  T  F  H  E  O  E  I  I  V
O  C  I  Z  O  A  W  K  I  S  S  N  T  N  H  A
S  C  R  E  A  M  E  S  F  Z  S  K  I  P  L  W
```

BEND	RIDE
BITE	SCRATCH
BLOW	SCREAM
BRUSH	SING
CLOSE	SKIP
FALL	SLIDE
HOP	STIR
KISS	STRETCH
OPEN	SWING
PLAY	WAVE
PULL	WHISTLE
PUSH	WINK

1) 2) 3) 4) 5) 6) 7) 8) 9) 10) 11) 12) 13) 14) 15) 16) 17) 18) 19) 20) 21) 22) 23) 24)

ANSWER KEY

DRAWINGS Page 4

1) scratch 2) fall 3) kiss 4) swing 5) skip 6) whistle 7) push 8) slide 9) pull 10) blow 11) bite 12) open 13) stretch 14) scream 15) hop 16) brush 17) ride 18) sing 19) close 20) play 21) bend 22) wink 23) wave 24) stir

ORDERING

1) bend 2) bite 3) blow 4) brush 5) close 6) fall 7) hop 8) kiss 9) open 10) play 11) pull 12) push 13) ride 14) scratch 15) scream 16) sing 17) skip 18) slide 19) stir 20) stretch 21) swing 22) wave 23) whistle 24) wink

QUIZ

1) a) pull b) open

2) ?

3) ?

DASHES

1) hop 2) stir 3) skip 4) whistle 5) ride 6) scratch 7) sing 8) pull 9) slide 10) push 11) brush 12) wink 13) scream 14) play 15) fall 16) bite 17) stretch 18) wave 19) blow 20) kiss 21) open 22) bend 23) close 24) swing

WORD SPIRAL

1) wave 2) kiss 3) fall 4) scratch 5) open 6) brush 7) whistle 8) skip 9) slide 10) hop 11) close 12) play 13) push 14) bite 15) sing 16) wink 17) pull 18) blow 19) scream 20) bend 21) stir 22) swing 23) stretch 24) ride

WORD MAZES

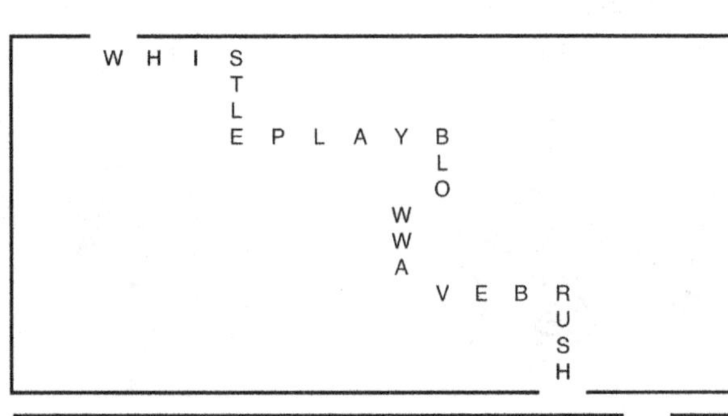

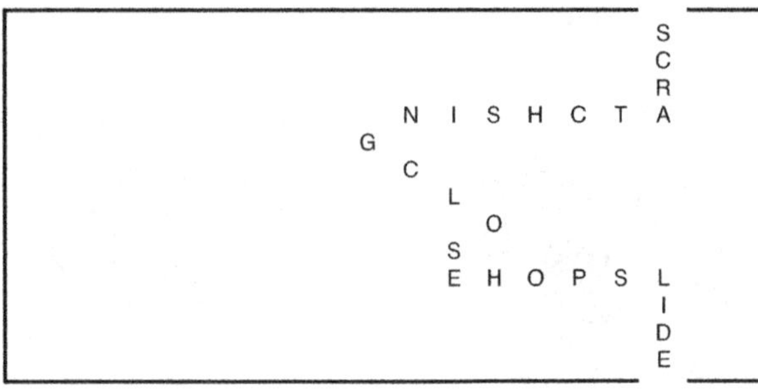

SCRAMBLES

1) wedding 2) muscles

EIGHT MISTAKES

1) soccer ball 2) top of baseball hat 3) skipping rope 4) half of flag 5) line from roof of school 6) football 7) collar on waving boy 8) bush in front of school

FIND-THE-WORDS PUZZLE

MAGIC WORD

1) slide 2) wink 3) swing 4) scream 5) ride 6) bend 7) bite 8) open 9) sing 10) whistle 11) brush   MAGIC WORD: ingredients

CROSSWORD PUZZLE

ACROSS: 1) brush 3) skip 5) fall 6) wink 7) stretch 9) scream 10) swing 12) ride 13) stir 14) wave 15) close 17) push 18) blow 19) bend   DOWN: 2) hop 3) slide 4) open 6) whistle 8) kiss 9) scratch 11) play 16) sing 17) pull 18) bite

TEST Page 13

1) wave 2) kiss 3) fall 4) scratch 5) open 6) brush 7) whistle 8) skip 9) slide 10) hop 11) close 12) play 13) push 14) bite 15) sing 16) wink 17) pull 18) blow 19) scream 20) bend 21) stir 22) swing 23) stretch 24) ride

Unit 9: Tools

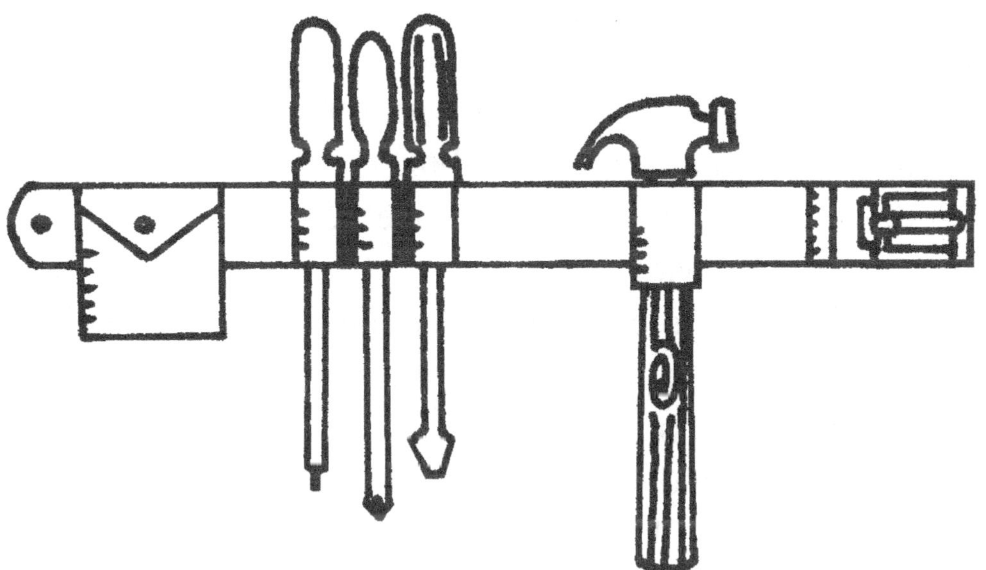

SENTENCES

1. A hammer is used to pound in a nail.
2. A rake is used to gather leaves.
3. I use a circular saw to cut wood quickly.
4. A screwdriver is used to insert or to take out a screw.
5. When I am working, I wear a tool belt around my waist.
6. We use a level to make sure that something is straight.
7. A shovel is used to dig a hole.
8. My father uses a sander to make surfaces smooth.
9. While the glue was drying, a clamp held the two pieces of wood together.
10. I used an extension cord because the electrical outlet was too far away.
11. My grandfather uses a hoe to weed his garden.
12. I have to fix a flat tire, but I can't loosen the nut.
13. My tools are organized in a toolbox.
14. A screw is used to fasten things together.
15. You make a hole with a drill.
16. The simplest way to cut something is to use a handsaw.
17. When I need to determine distance, I use a tape measure.
18. An ax is used to chop wood.
19. A nut fits on the end of a bolt.
20. When you drill a hole, the size of the hole is determined by the drill bit.
21. Pliers can remove a rusty nail from a piece of wood.
22. When building a chair, a staple gun is used to fasten the upholstery.
23. The carpenter hammered the nail into the wood.
24. A wrench is used to loosen or tighten nuts and bolts.

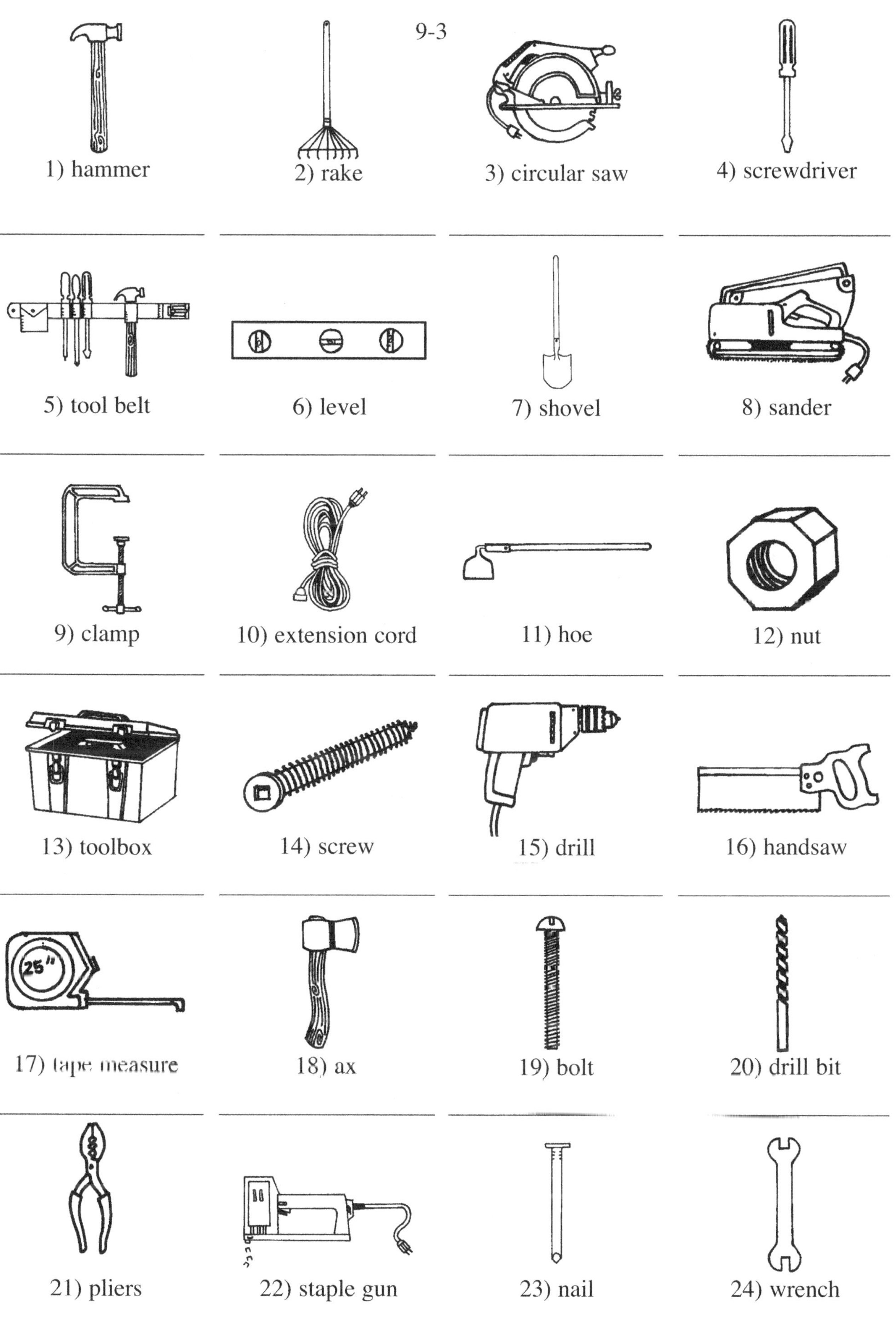

9-3
1) hammer
2) rake
3) circular saw
4) screwdriver
5) tool belt
6) level
7) shovel
8) sander
9) clamp
10) extension cord
11) hoe
12) nut
13) toolbox
14) screw
15) drill
16) handsaw
17) tape measure
18) ax
19) bolt
20) drill bit
21) pliers
22) staple gun
23) nail
24) wrench

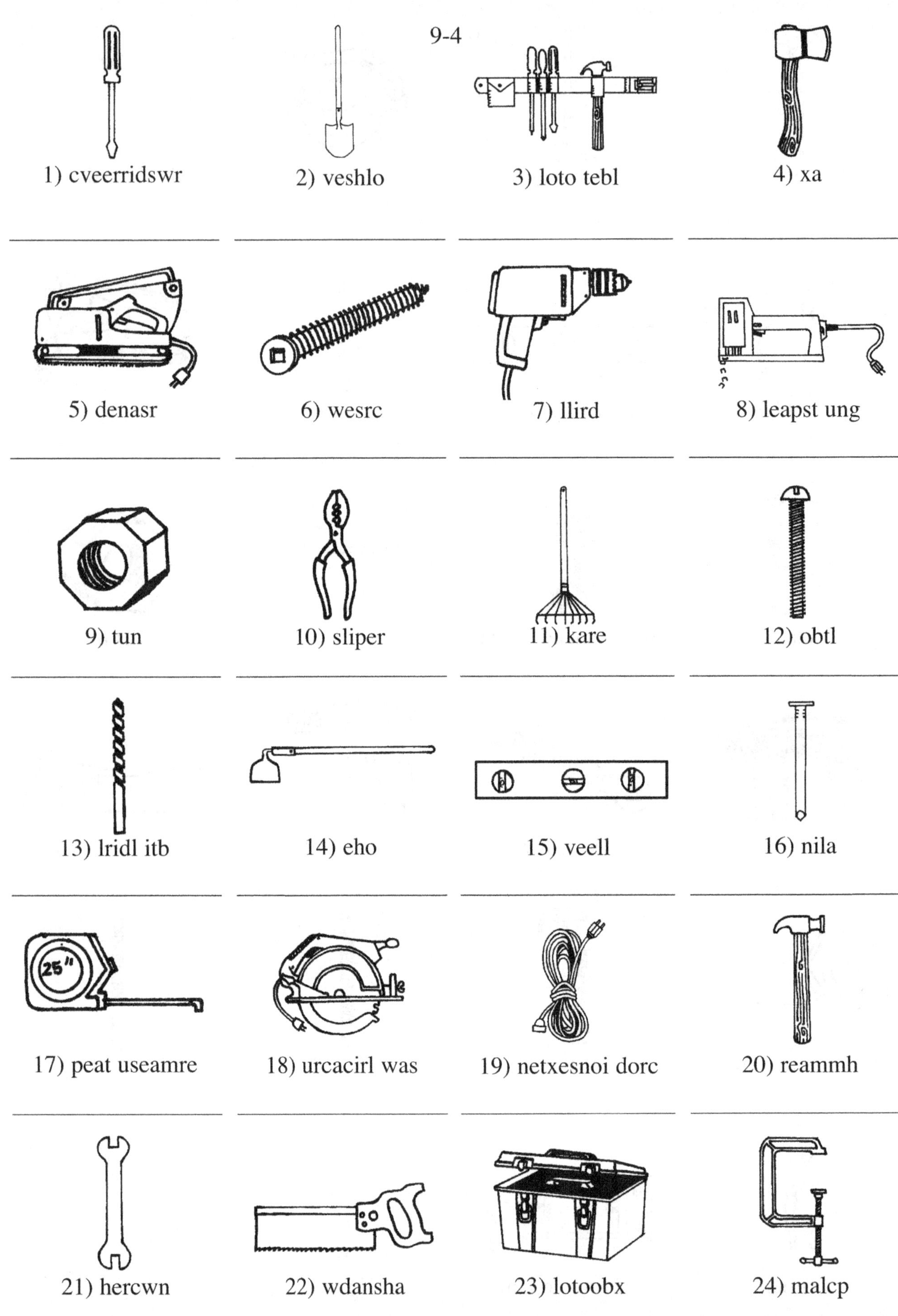

9-4
1) cveerridswr
2) veshlo
3) loto tebl
4) xa
5) denasr
6) wesrc
7) llird
8) leapst ung
9) tun
10) sliper
11) kare
12) obtl
13) lridl itb
14) eho
15) veell
16) nila
17) peat useamre
18) urcacirl was
19) netxesnoi dorc
20) reammh
21) hercwn
22) wdansha
23) lotoobx
24) malcp

ORDERING

Put the words in alphabetical order.

screwdriver	handsaw	extension cord	tool belt
hammer	drill bit	toolbox	staple gun
wrench	bolt	ax	shovel
rake	sander	level	screw
hoe	circular saw	clamp	nail
drill	pliers	tape measure	nut

1) _______________________   13) _______________________

2) _______________________   14) _______________________

3) _______________________   15) _______________________

4) _______________________   16) _______________________

5) _______________________   17) _______________________

6) _______________________   18) _______________________

7) _______________________   19) _______________________

8) _______________________   20) _______________________

9) _______________________   21) _______________________

10) _______________________   22) _______________________

11) _______________________   23) _______________________

12) _______________________   24) _______________________

QUIZ

1) List all of the compound words.

____

2) What other tool can you make using some of the letters in the word a) shovel?
   b) staple gun? c) toolbox?

____

3) Which tool is spelled the same way both forward and backward?

____

DASHES

Complete each word by adding the missing letters. Each dash represents a letter.

1) d r _ _ _
2) s _ r _ w _ r _ v _ r
3) h _ _ d _ _ w
4) h _ _ m _ _
5) s _ n _ e _
6) w _ _ n _ h
7) c _ _ c _ _ a _   s _ w
8) r _ _ e
9) p _ _ e _ s
10) h _ _
11) e _ _ e _ _ i _ _   c _ _ d
12) d _ _ l _   b _ _

13) s _ _ p _ e   g _ n
14) t o _ _ b _ _
15) s _ o _ e _
16) a _
17) s _ r _ _
18) l _ _ e _
19) n _ _ l
20) c l _ _ _
21) n _ _
22) t a _ _   m _ a _ u _ e
23) b _ _ t
24) t _ _ l   b _ _ t

WORD SPIRAL

Following the spiral towards the center, circle all the vocabulary words from this unit.

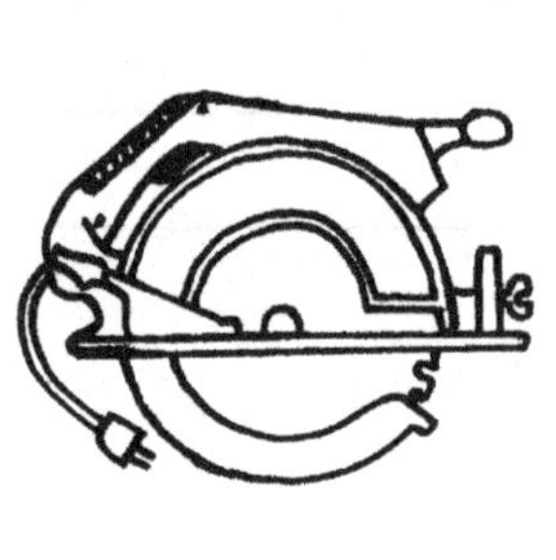

SCRAMBLES

Unscramble the jumbled letters to form words from this unit. Arrange the circled letters to form a surprise answer.

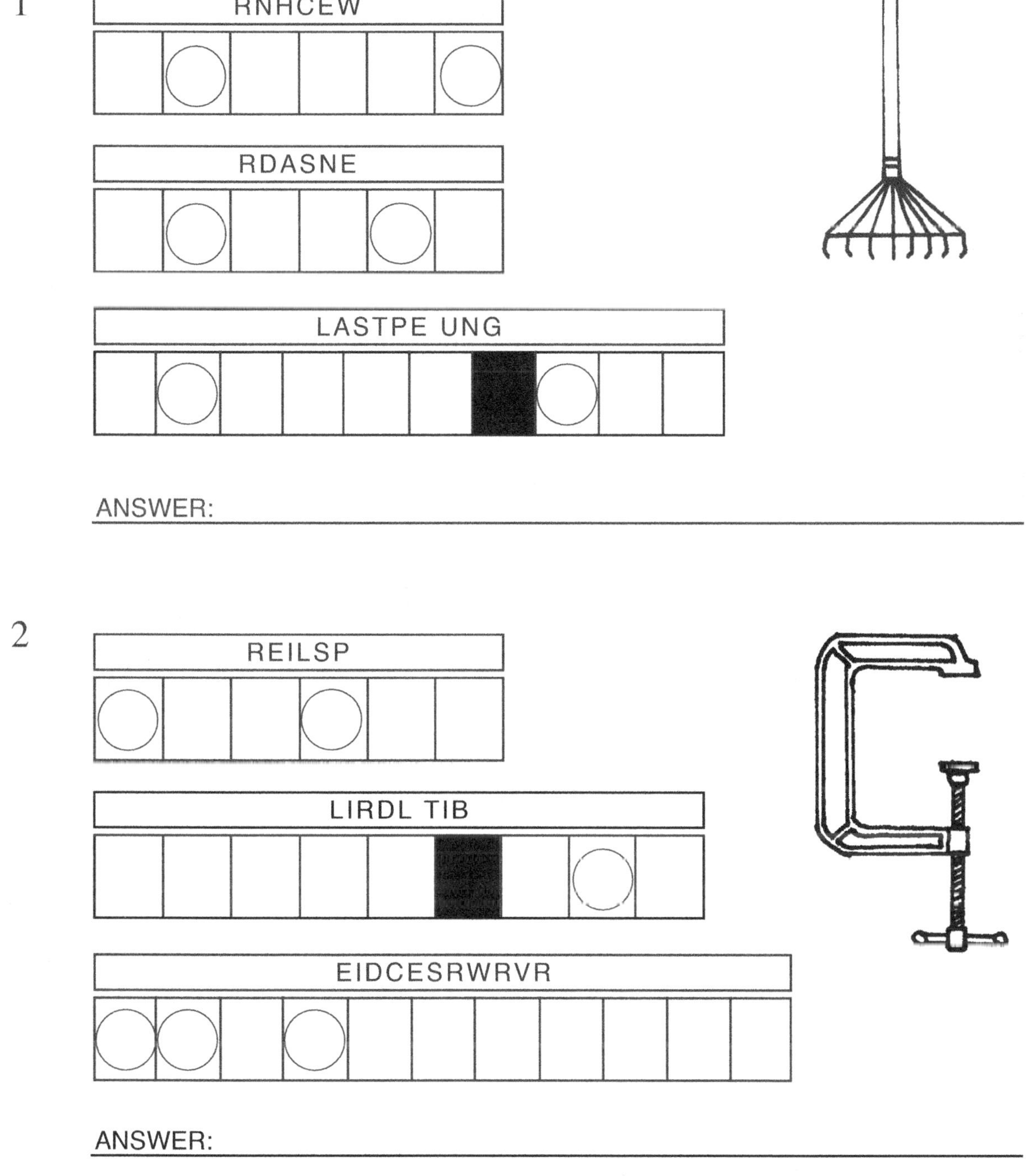

1

RNHCEW

RDASNE

LASTPE UNG

ANSWER: _______________________________________

2

REILSP

LIRDL TIB

EIDCESRWRVR

ANSWER: _______________________________________

WORD MAZES

To find your way out of each maze, follow words from the unit from START to FINISH. The words can go from left-to-right, from right-to-left, upward, downward or diagonally.

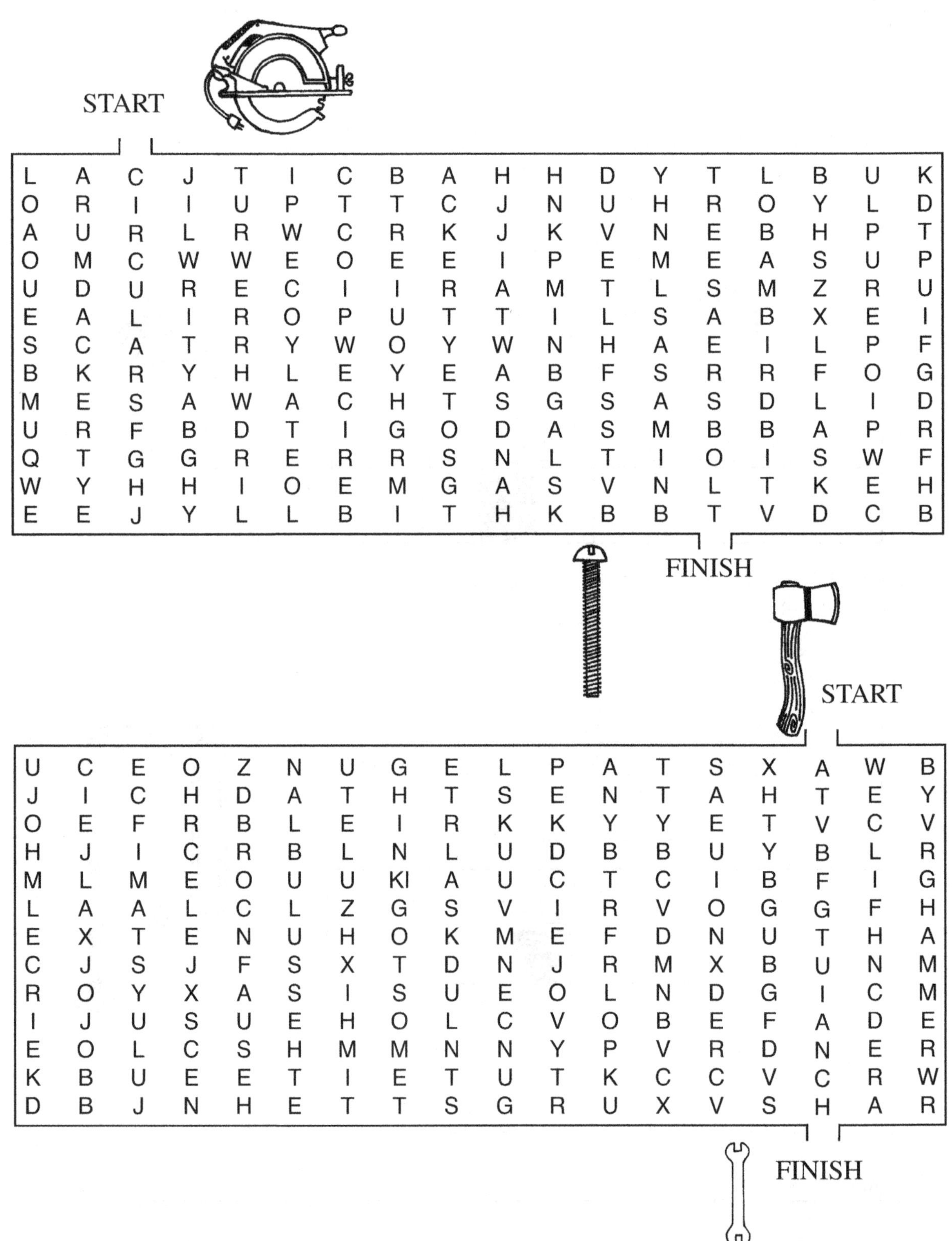

MAGIC WORD

Using words from the unit, complete the fill in the blanks exercise below. When you fill in those words on the chart an extra word will appear in the box.

1) ___ ___ ___ ___ ___ | ___ | ___ ___ ___ ___ ___

2) ___ ___ ___ | ___ | ___ ___

3) ___ ___ | ___

4) ___ ___ ___ ___ | ___ | ___

5) ___ | ___ ___ ___ ___ ___

6) ___ ___ | ___ | ___ ___ ___

7) ___ ___ | ___ | ___ ___

8) ___ ___ | ___ | ___ ___ ___

9) ___ | ___ | ___ ___ ___

1) A _____________________ is used to insert or to take out a screw.

2) _____________________ can remove a rusty nail from a piece of wood.

3) I have to fix a flat tire, but I can't loosen the _____________________.

4) A _____________________ is used to dig a hole.

5) A _____________________ is used to loosen or tighten nuts and bolts.

6) A _____________________ is used to pound in a nail.

7) You make a hole with a _____________________.

8) My father uses a _____________________ to make surfaces smooth.

9) We use a _____________________ to make sure that something is straight.

MAGIC WORD: _____________________

EIGHT MISTAKES

There are 8 things missing from Picture Two that can be found in Picture One. Find the missing items and write them down.

1 ____

2 ____

3 ____

4 ____

5 ____

6 ____

7 ____

8 ____

CROSSWORD PUZZLE

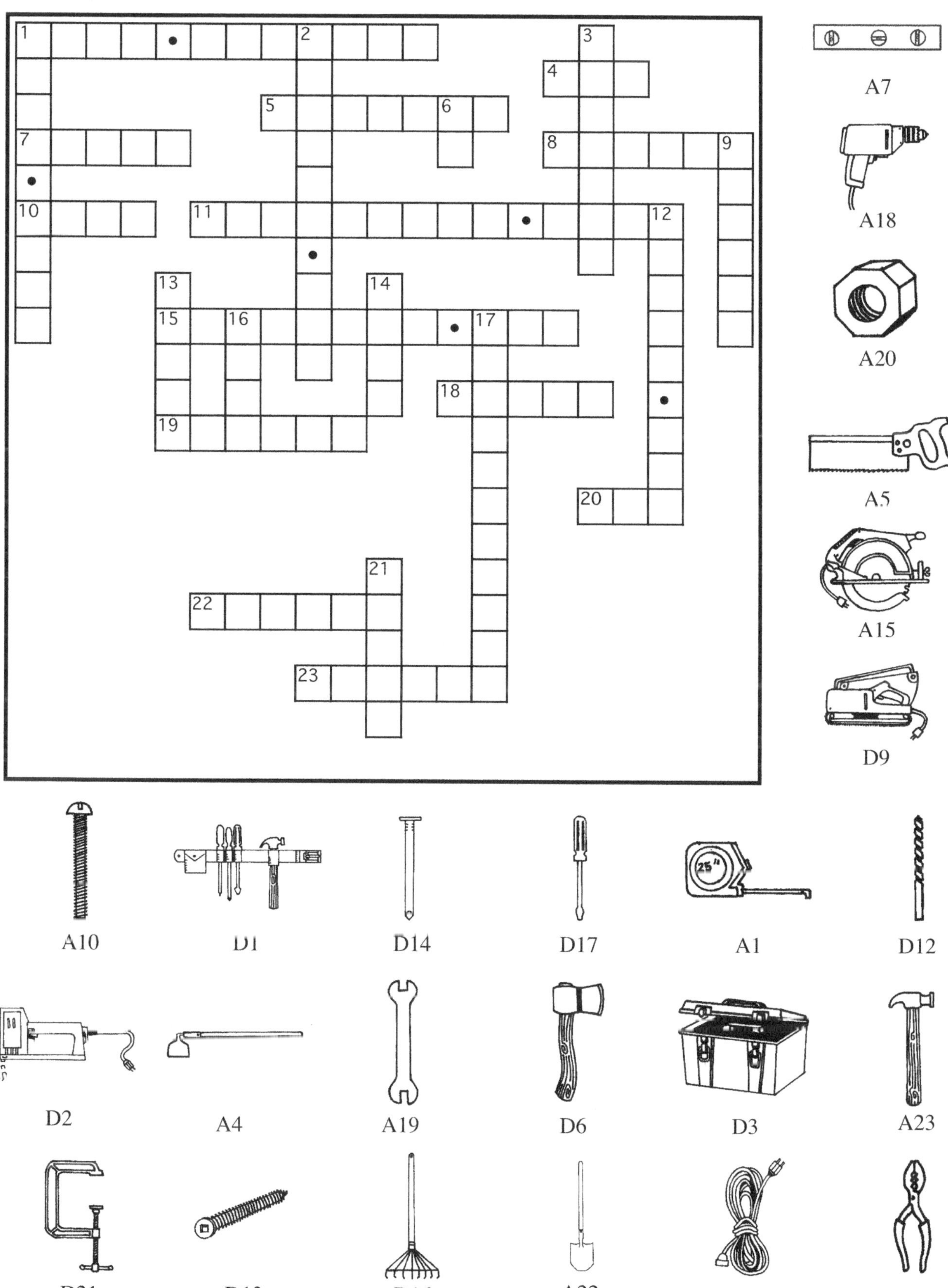

FIND-THE-WORDS PUZZLE

You will find all the words from this unit hidden in the box below. Find each word and circle all its letters. To find the words you may have to read from left-to-right, from right-to-left, upward, downward or diagonally.

R	E	V	I	R	D	W	E	R	C	S	T	O	A	E	A
S	X	Y	A	V	A	R	N	U	G	E	L	P	A	T	S
N	T	A	P	E	M	E	A	S	U	R	E	N	L	A	R
D	E	W	N	E	X	O	B	L	O	O	T	H	R	R	E
A	N	A	O	R	R	H	C	N	E	R	W	A	I	T	I
U	S	S	D	Y	Y	N	A	W	O	T	U	N	A	I	L
B	I	H	T	R	E	M	M	A	H	I	Y	D	G	I	P
T	O	E	S	O	I	A	R	E	L	G	U	S	H	S	N
L	N	R	O	R	G	L	L	F	O	H	O	A	T	I	D
E	C	C	I	R	C	U	L	A	R	S	A	W	Y	N	S
B	O	T	L	O	B	M	I	X	V	A	R	N	O	G	S
L	R	N	E	A	I	E	N	L	E	N	E	A	R	H	M
O	D	A	V	D	M	A	G	L	T	D	G	B	O	O	E
O	R	M	E	I	R	P	I	I	O	E	O	V	H	K	A
T	E	E	L	N	L	D	F	N	N	R	E	E	A	D	R
W	E	R	C	S	O	T	I	B	L	L	I	R	D	H	C

AX	NUT
BOLT	PLIERS
CIRCULAR SAW	RAKE
CLAMP	SANDER
DRILL	SCREW
DRILL BIT	SCREWDRIVER
EXTENSION CORD	SHOVEL
HAMMER	STAPLE GUN
HANDSAW	TAPE MEASURE
HOE	TOOL BELT
LEVEL	TOOLBOX
NAIL	WRENCH

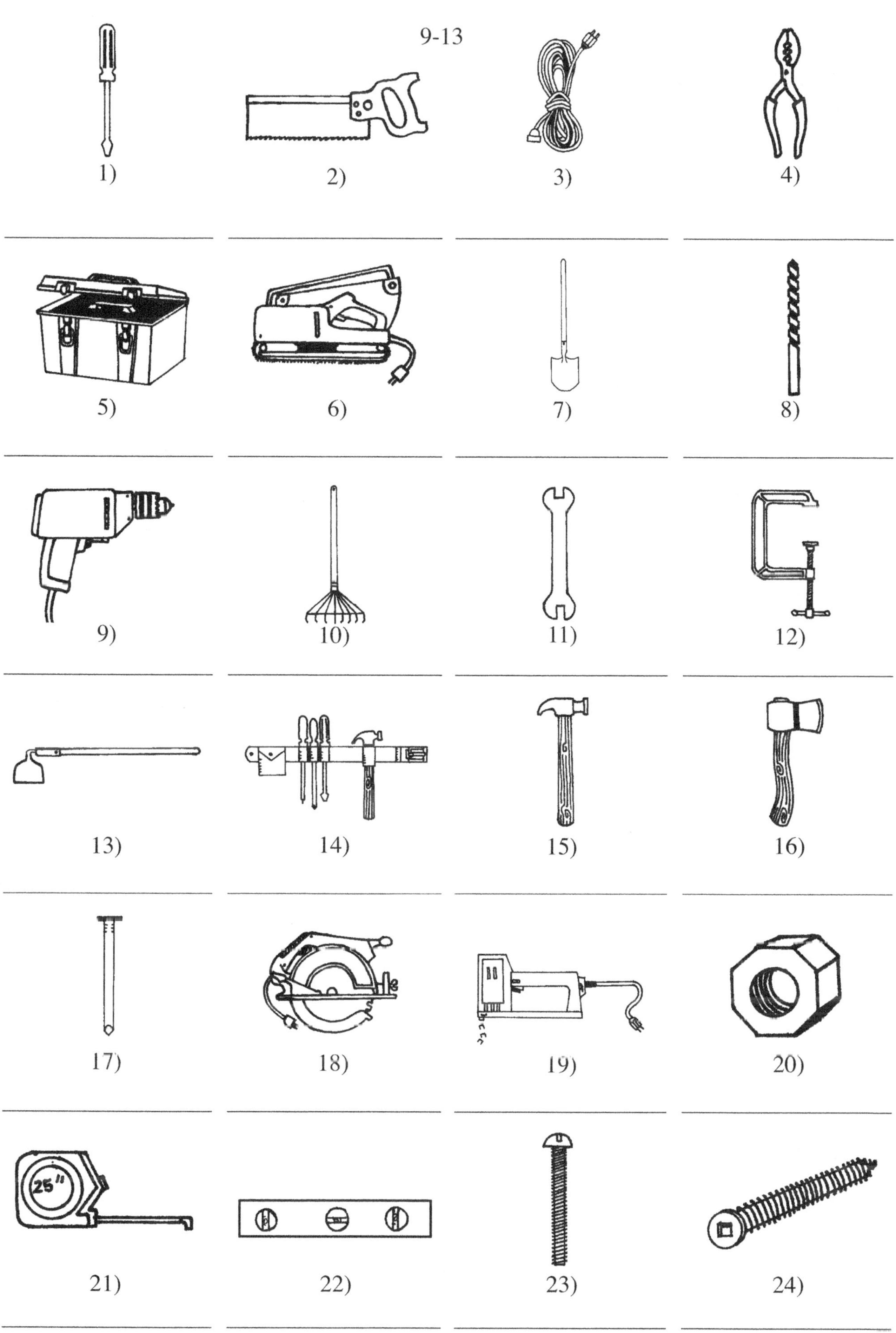

1)
2)
3)
4)
5)
6)
7)
8)
9)
10)
11)
12)
13)
14)
15)
16)
17)
18)
19)
20)
21)
25"
22)
23)
24)

ANSWER KEY

DRAWINGS Page 4

1) screwdriver 2) shovel 3) tool belt 4) ax 5) sander 6) screw 7) drill 8) staple gun 9) nut 10) pliers 11) rake 12) bolt 13) drill bit 14) hoe 15) level 16) nail 17) tape measure 18) circular saw 19) extension cord 20) hammer 21) wrench 22) handsaw 23) toolbox 24) clamp

ORDERING

1) ax 2) bolt 3) circular saw 4) clamp 5) drill 6) drill bit 7) extension cord 8) hammer 9) handsaw 10) hoe 11) level 12) nail 13) nut 14) pliers 15) rake 16) sander 17) screw 18) screwdriver 19) shovel 20) staple gun 21) tape measure 22) tool belt 23) toolbox 24) wrench

QUIZ

1) screwdriver, handsaw, toolbox

2) a) hoe b) nut c) bolt

3) level

DASHES

1) drill 2) screwdriver 3) handsaw 4) hammer 5) sander 6) wrench 7) circular saw 8) rake 9) pliers 10) hoe 11) extension cord 12) drill bit 13) staple gun 14) toolbox 15) shovel 16) ax 17) screw 18) level 19) nail 20) clamp 21) nut 22) tape measure 23) bolt 24) tool belt

WORD SPIRAL

1) screwdriver 2) handsaw 3) extension cord 4) pliers 5) toolbox 6) sander 7) shovel 8) drill bit 9) drill 10) rake 11) wrench 12) clamp 13) hoe 14) tool belt 15) hammer 16) ax 17) nail 18) circular saw 19) staple gun 20) bolt 21) tape measure 22) level 23) nut 24) screw

WORD MAZES

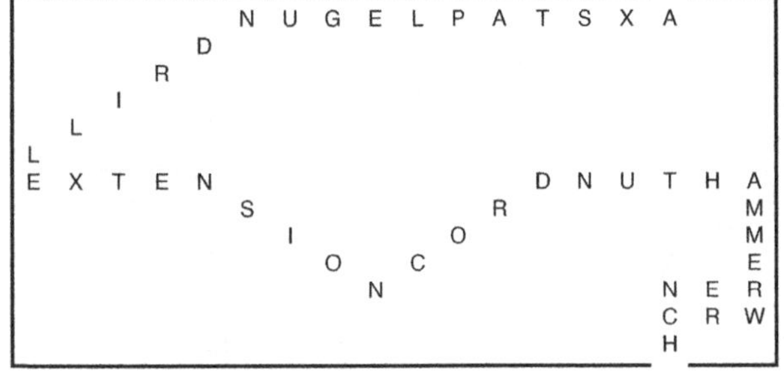

SCRAMBLES

1) gather 2) pieces

EIGHT MISTAKES

1) middle of work bench 2) bolt on support holding up man with drill 3) nail being hit by man with hammer 4) screwdriver is shorter 5) right ear of the man with the drill 6) tongue of man sawing 7) wrench from pocket of man with drill 8) bottom left hand bird

FIND-THE-WORDS PUZZLE

MAGIC WORD

1) screwdriver 2) pliers 3) nut 4) shovel 5) wrench 6) hammer 7) drill 8) sander 9) level   MAGIC WORD: determine

CROSSWORD PUZZLE

ACROSS: 1) tape measure 4) hoe 5) handsaw 7) level 8) pliers 10) bolt 11) extension cord 15) circular saw 18) drill 19) wrench 20) nut 22) shovel 23) hammer   DOWN: 1) tool belt 2) staple gun 3) toolbox 6) ax 9) sander 12) drill bit 13) screw 14) nail 16) rake 17) screwdriver 21) clamp

TEST Page 13

1) screwdriver 2) handsaw 3) extension cord 4) pliers 5) toolbox 6) sander 7) shovel 8) drill bit 9) drill 10) rake 11) wrench 12) clamp 13) hoe 14) tool belt 15) hammer 16) ax 17) nail 18) circular saw 19) staple gun 20) nut 21) tape measure 22) level 23) bolt 24) screw

Unit 10: Daily Activities

SENTENCES

1. I do not like talking in front of large audiences.
2. My mother goes walking every morning.
3. I love to spend time watching old movies.
4. I need a break because I've been working all day.
5. I like spending my spare time playing video games.
6. He is sleeping like a baby.
7. Waking some mornings is a difficult thing!
8. I start every day by washing my face.
9. I'll be ready to go to the party after I finish combing my hair.
10. My older sister spends half the night phoning her friends.
11. Listening to music is a great way of relaxing.
12. What are you thinking about right now?
13. My youngest child still needs help dressing himself in the morning.
14. My mom is cleaning our house because we have guests arriving soon.
15. Make sure that you separate the whites and colors when you do laundry.
16. I start the day by reading the local newspaper.
17. Driving the speed limit is the safest way to drive.
18. Whenever my wife and I do the dishes, she washes and I dry.
19. I'm brushing my teeth because I want my breath to smell nice.
20. I have been exercising because I want to stay in shape.
21. I'm going to start eating more vegetables.
22. I like drinking a glass of cold water when I return from jogging.
23. I'm cooking dinner because it is my mother's birthday.
24. The phone always rings when I am bathing.

1) talking

2) walking

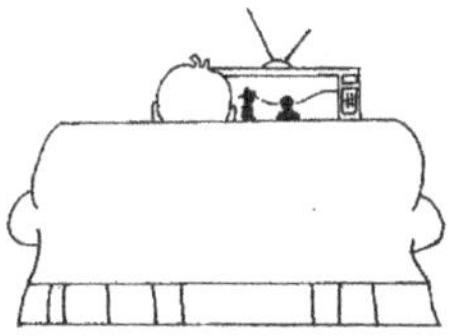

3) watching

4) working

5) playing

6) sleeping

7) waking

8) washing

9) combing

10) phoning

11) relaxing

12) thinking

13) dressing

14) cleaning

15) laundry

16) reading

17) driving

18) dishes

19) brushing

20) exercising

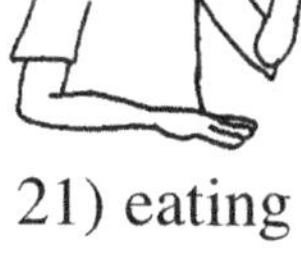

21) eating

22) drinking

23) cooking

24) bathing

1) shides

2) neatgi

3) ikocogn

4) tabignh

5) gelacnin

6) nvirdig

7) sirexiceng

8) ikirnngd

9) ginrowk

10) dsisenrg

11) rigenad

12) husirbgn

13) gnawik

14) chatingw

15) nniikthg

16) lynadur

17) nobgimc

18) legenisp

19) lawnikg

20) xragnile

21) hingopn

22) hawnigs

23) aginply

24) gailtkn

ORDERING

Put the words in alphabetical order.

combing	dishes	laundry	thinking
brushing	washing	cleaning	watching
reading	drinking	dressing	relaxing
cooking	bathing	driving	waking
eating	phoning	walking	playing
sleeping	exercising	talking	working

1) _______________________

2) _______________________

3) _______________________

4) _______________________

5) _______________________

6) _______________________

7) _______________________

8) _______________________

9) _______________________

10) _______________________

11) _______________________

12) _______________________

13) _______________________

14) _______________________

15) _______________________

16) _______________________

17) _______________________

18) _______________________

19) _______________________

20) _______________________

21) _______________________

22) _______________________

23) _______________________

24) _______________________

QUIZ

1) List those daily activities that you have already done today.

____

2) The letters 'ph' in the word *phoning* make the same sound as what letter? Can you think of other words that use 'ph' in the same way?

____

3) In the word *combing*, what letter is silent? Can you think of other words that have the same silent letter?

____

DASHES

Complete each word by adding the missing letters. Each dash represents a letter.

1) c _ _ _ i n g

2) d _ _ h _ _

3) b _ u _ _ i _ g

4) w _ _ h i _ _

5) r _ _ d _ _ g

6) d r i _ _ i _ _

7) c o _ _ i _ g

8) b _ _ h _ _ g

9) e _ _ i _ _

10) p _ _ n _ _ g

11) s _ _ e _ _ n g

12) e _ _ r _ _ s i _ _

13) l _ u _ d _ y

14) w _ _ i n g

15) c _ _ a _ _ n g

16) w _ r _ _ _ g

17) d _ _ s _ i _ g

18) p _ _ y _ _ g

19) d r _ _ _ n g

20) r _ l _ x _ n _

21) w a _ _ i n _

22) t _ _ k _ _ g

23) w _ _ c _ _ n g

24) t _ _ n _ _ n g

WORD SPIRAL

Following the spiral towards the center, circle all the vocabulary words from this unit.

SCRAMBLES

Unscramble the jumbled letters to form words from this unit. Arrange the circled letters to form a surprise answer.

1

GIMCOBN

GIAETN

RNALUDY

ANSWER: ____

2

NHAWSIG

GISRBUHN

NDERAIG

ANSWER: ____

WORD MAZES

To find your way out of each maze, follow words from the unit from START to FINISH.
The words can go from left-to-right, from right-to-left, upward, downward or diagonally.

START

```
K I C L A W A T K A T U O G O I F A
L U O O R G H D C A S R I D I P S C
S O M A U N N U U H F W P Y W N G T
A Y B O M I U V L F I E W A E E E C
S H I U D S H M P G I N E L C C A O
A G N E A I M N N H B R G P O A T I
M R G S C C I E E J U H K V Y A I P
I M E X E R N R R J E N D L O L N W
N N I M E B B T T I B I K O A C G E
B V G U R I G F R L G N P I T T U C
T C F Q T T A L E W H G U I E T S I
R X E W Y V L E S R Y S L E E P I R
E D Q E E B S B A I T C F Y O G N E
```

FINISH

START

```
H E L S P O E N A S S A A L R D F I
E K W Y A R C I R K K A L P R H G N
E D R U Y U F I T U A E B I R A H B
H C I L L T A T F U U D N Y G S I S
I I T U D H U E D V L K L N A A A H
N E G J E I S L I M I G I S S A T E
B J L O A S E U T N N H J K K A W S
A Y R D N U A L G E T J O D I A J S
D R S M O O T H W A R J H U N S I K
F E L A X I N G B T A I M V G D R E
C E U I Y O D O G F R K S T R O E S
R N V L F B I W A L E N B N N N I S
I Z E L F B D H L A S G L E E G H P
```

FINISH

MAGIC WORD

Using words from the unit, complete the fill in the blanks exercise below. When you fill in those words on the chart an extra word will appear in the box.

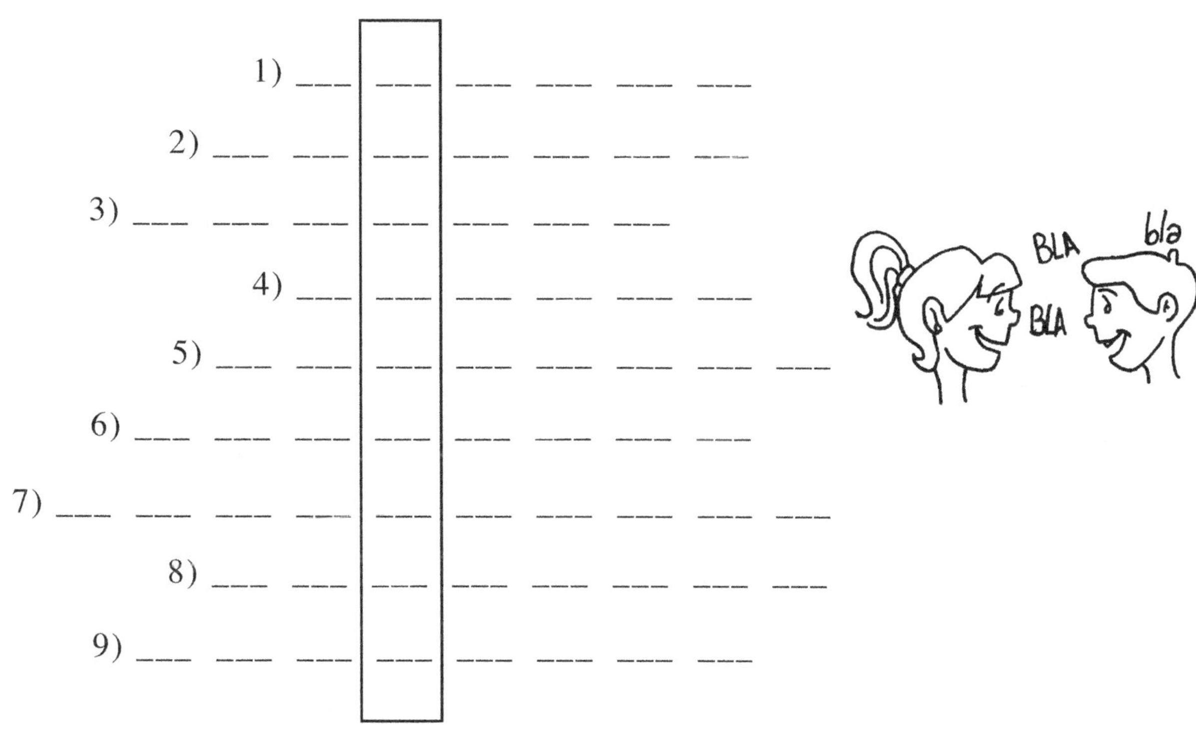

1) I'm going to start ___________________ more vegetables.

2) Make sure that you separate the whites and colors when you do ___________________.

3) I start the day by ___________________ the local newspaper.

4) Whenever my wife and I do the ___________________, she washes and I dry.

5) My mom is ___________________ our house because we have guests arriving soon.

6) What are you _________ _________ about right now?

7) I have been _________________ because I want to stay in shape.

8) My youngest child still needs help ___________________ himself in the morning.

9) I'm ___________________ my teeth because I want my breath to smell nice.

MAGIC WORD: ___________________

EIGHT MISTAKES

There are 8 things missing from Picture Two that can be found in Picture One. Find the missing items and write them down.

1 ____

2 ____

3 ____

4 ____

5 ____

6 ____

7 ____

8 ____

CROSSWORD PUZZLE

FIND-THE-WORDS PUZZLE

You will find all the words from this unit hidden in the box below. Find each word and circle all its letters. To find the words you may have to read from left-to-right, from right-to-left, upward, downward or diagonally.

```
R F E D R I N K I N G X V T H G
E R R R T A G N I H S U R B S N
L I F E N W C O F E A U G L E I
A W D S D B A T H I N G K A H H
X A T S W T C C A U P B I U S C
I L V I A C O A D L H H B N I T
N K T N S R M U A H O U C D D A
G I A G H Q B Y D G N I K R O W
S N S T I G I G O A I O D Y O T
G G L D N N N N C G N T R O L D
N C E L G I G I G N G N I K A W
I A E D K N F K N I U F V H P M
K Z P N W A R O I D I G I R P U
L A I O T E V O T A N H N A Q G
A H N X L L V C A E F H G B R L
T S G E L C E X E R C I S I N G
```

BATHING	PHONING
BRUSHING	PLAYING
CLEANING	READING
COMBING	RELAXING
COOKING	SLEEPING
DISHES	TALKING
DRESSING	THINKING
DRINKING	WAKING
DRIVING	WALKING
EATING	WASHING
EXERCISING	WATCHING
LAUNDRY	WORKING

1)

2)

3)

4)

5)

6)

7)

8)

9)

10)

11)

12)

13)

14)

15)

16)

17)

18)

19)

20)

21)

22)

23)

24)

ANSWER KEY

DRAWINGS Page 4

1) dishes 2) eating 3) cooking 4) bathing 5) cleaning 6) driving 7) exercising 8) drinking 9) working 10) dressing 11) reading 12) brushing 13) waking 14) watching 15) thinking 16) laundry 17) combing 18) sleeping 19) walking 20) relaxing 21) phoning 22) washing 23) playing 24) talking

ORDERING

1) bathing 2) brushing 3) cleaning 4) combing 5) cooking 6) dishes 7) dressing 8) drinking 9) driving 10) eating 11) exercising 12) laundry 13) phoning 14) playing 15) reading 16) relaxing 17) sleeping 18) talking 19) thinking 20) waking 21) walking 22) washing 23) watching 24) working

QUIZ

1) ?
2) F; examples include phrase, phantom, pharoah, phonics, pharmacy, pheasant, philosophy, physics, phobia, phoenix, photo
3) B; examples include climb, dumb, crumb, tomb, womb, bomb

DASHES

1) combing 2) dishes 3) brushing 4) washing 5) reading 6) drinking 7) cooking 8) bathing 9) eating 10) phoning 11) sleeping 12) exercising 13) laundry 14) waking 15) cleaning 16) working 17) dressing 18) playing 19) driving 20) relaxing 21) walking 22) talking 23) watching 24) thinking

WORD SPIRAL

1) driving 2) exercising 3) bathing 4) dishes 5) working 6) reading 7) brushing 8) cooking 9) watching 10) cleaning 11) laundry 12) drinking 13) combing 14) walking 15) dressing 16) thinking 17) washing 18) waking 19) talking 20) relaxing 21) eating 22) phoning 23) sleeping 24) playing

WORD MAZES

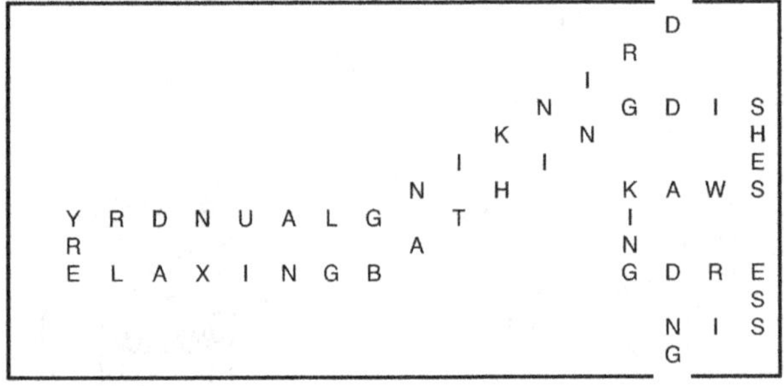

SCRAMBLES

1) morning 2) husband

EIGHT MISTAKES

1) pickle from jar 2) slice of bread 3) line on boy's cheek 4) steam from roast 5) cupboard door handle 6) man's shoe 7) middle of girl's plate 8) radio antenna

FIND-THE-WORDS PUZZLE

MAGIC WORD

1) eating 2) laundry 3) reading 4) dishes 5) cleaning 6) thinking 7) exercising 8) dressing 9) brushing MAGIC WORD: audiences

CROSSWORD PUZZLE

ACROSS: 1) cooking 4) walking 5) waking 6) brushing 8) drinking 9) exercising 13) thinking 15) dressing 17) working 18) laundry 19) playing 20) cleaning   DOWN: 1) combing 2) watching 3) washing 6) bathing 7) sleeping 8) driving 10) relaxing 11) dishes 12) eating 13) talking 14) phoning 16) reading

TEST Page 13

1) driving 2) exercising 3) dishes 4) bathing 5) working 6) reading 7) brushing 8) cooking 9) watching 10) cleaning 11) laundry 12) drinking 13) combing 14) walking 15) dressing 16) thinking 17) washing 18) waking 19) talking 20) relaxing 21) eating 22) phoning 23) sleeping 24) playing

Made in the USA
Monee, IL
07 July 2026